The Dark Masters

*Vivo: The Life of
Gustav Meyrink*

To olive and Arthur
Our friendly neighbourhood watch

Mike Mitchell

Mike

Vivo: The Life of Gustav Meyrink

Dedalus

Published in the UK by Dedalus Limited
24–26, St Judith's Lane, Sawtry, Cambs, PE28 5XE
email: info@dedalusbooks.com
www.dedalusbooks.com

ISBN 978 1 903517 69 7

Dedalus is distributed in the USA by SCB Distributors
15608 South New Century Drive, Gardena, CA 90248
email: info@scbdistributors.com   web: www.scbdistributors.com

Dedalus is distributed in Australia by Peribo Pty Ltd.
58, Beaumont Road, Mount Kuring-gai, N.S.W. 2080
email: info@peribo.com.au

Dedalus is distributed in Canada by Disticor Direct-Book Division
695, Westney Road South, Suite 14, Ajax, Ontario, LI6 6M9
email: ndalton@disticor.com   web: www.disticordirect.com

First published by Dedalus in 2008

Printed in Finland by WS Bookwell
Typeset by RefineCatch Limited, Bungay, Suffolk

ABOUT THE AUTHOR

For many years an academic with a special interest in Austrian literature, Mike Mitchell taught German at Stirling University, taking early retirement in 1995 to concentrate on his work as a translator. As well as the five novels of Meyrink, he has translated a wide range of German authors, from Grimmelshausen to Goethe, Oskar Kokoschka, Alfred Kubin and Helmut Krausser; his translation of Herbert Rosendorfer's *Letters Back to Ancient China* was awarded the 1998 Schlegel-Tieck prize.

ACKNOWLEDGEMENTS

The author would like to thank the following for the supply of material:

Munich City Library for photographs: 5, 11, 12 and frontispiece.
Frankfurt University Library for photograph 1.

Despite the best efforts of the author, it has not proved possible to identify the sources of all the photographs used in this edition. We would be grateful, therefore, if any rights holders would contact Dedalus.

I would also like to thank the following for making archive material available:

> the Kubin Archive in the Lenbachhaus Gallery, Munich;
> the Goethe-Schiller Archive, Marbach;
> the Monacensia Archive of Munich City Library;
> the Bavarian State Library, Munich – unless otherwise indicated, letters, manuscripts and documents quoted from are in the Meyrinkiana in the Manuscript Department of the Bavarian State Library.
> Dundee University Library for the supply of journal photocopies.

I am grateful to the authors of the German biographies of Meyrink: Eduard Frank: *Gustav Meyrink: Werk und Wirkung*, Manfred Lube: *Gustav Meyrink: Beiträge zur Biographie und Studien zu seiner Kunsttheorie*, Mohammad Qasim: *Gustav*

Meyrink: Eine monographische Untersuchung, Frans Smit: *Gustav Meyrink: Auf der Suche nach dem Übersinnlichen* (originally in Dutch). I have made uninhibited use of their researches to support my own.

Page numbers of quotations from the above will be given, after the first occurrence, in brackets after the text; the translations are my own. The same will apply to works by Meyrink: quotations will be from the published translations; where these do not exist, the first reference will give the German title, with an English translation in brackets; further references will use the translated title. For essays and stories reference will be given to the anthology in which they are collected.

The private Meyrinkiana collections of Robert Karle, Lambert Binder and Eduard Frank are now in the Bibliotheca Philosophica Hermetica, Amsterdam.

CONTENTS

Prefatory note

Especially in his early years, Gustav Meyrink enjoyed a notoriety which, as Josef Strelka suggests[1] matched that of any of
the characters from his novels.

Unfortunately there is a dearth of documentary evidence.
Meyrink did not keep a diary, nor did he keep the personal
letters he received; most of those surviving relate to his dealings with occult societies and with publishers; relatively few
personal letters from Meyrink exist, most is business correspondence such as that with his publisher, Kurt Wolff, in
Yale University Library.

On the other hand, there is a wealth of *anecdote* about
Meyrink, much of it published after his death, and much of it
recounting fantastic events. How much of this is true is difficult to assess, but what it does attest is Meyrink's notorious
reputation in fin-de-siècle society in Prague and Munich.

The aim of this biography, then, is to provide the reader
with the facts of Meyrink's life, as far as they are ascertainable,
but also to give the reader some idea of Meyrink as he appeared
to his contemporaries, especially the younger contemporaries
who gathered round him.

To this end I have tried, as far as possible, to let Meyrink and
his acquaintances speak in their own voices and I hope this
will make accessible to the English-speaking reader much
material which has so far only been available in German.

[1] Gustav Meyrink: *Der Engel vom westlichen Fenster*, selected and with an
introduction by Josef Strelka, Graz, 1966, p. 7.

1

Birth and childhood

Meyrink was illegitimate.

He was born on 19 January 1868 in the Blauer Bock hotel in the Mariahilferstrasse in Vienna. Seven weeks later he was christened 'Gustav Meyer' in the Protestant church in the same street in Vienna.

His mother, Marie Meyer (she was christened Maria Wilhelmine Adelheide but used the name 'Marie' professionally), was an actress. At the time of Meyrink's birth she was 27 and engaged at the court theatre in Stuttgart.[1] She was described as 'temporarily resident' in Vienna; presumably she had gone there for the birth in order to avoid scandal. Her elder sister, Dustmann-Meyer, had been a singer at the Vienna Court Opera since 1857. Perhaps her sister's presence in the city was the reason Marie Meyer chose Vienna.

Meyrink's father was a wealthy aristocrat, Baron Friedrich Karl Gottlieb Varnbüler von und zu Hemmingen. Aged 59, he was also much older that his mistress. In the course of his career he occupied various important positions in the Württemberg administration (Stuttgart was the capital of Württemberg); at the time of Meyrink's birth he was foreign minister and president of the privy council, and in 1866 he had played a significant role in the Austro-Prussian conflict. He died in 1889. Although official acknowledgment was doubtless out of the question – as well as being an aristocrat,

---

[1] Staatsarchiv Ludwigsburg, E18 II Bü 660.

Varnbüler was also married – he appears to have deposited a large sum for his son, the interest from which his mother used to help finance his education. According to Alfred Schmid Noerr, a younger friend of Meyrink, in 1919, at the height of his fame as a writer, the Varnbülers offered to acknowledge him as a member of the family, but he refused.

An unpublished chronicle written by one of Marie Meyer's uncles,[2] claims the family had noble origins, came from Bavaria and was originally called Meyerink, but had changed their name to Meyer by the end of the seventeenth century. By the end of the eighteenth century the Meyers were settled in Hamburg, where Meyrink's grandfather was born. Both of Meyrink's grandparents, who were married in Aachen in 1831, worked in the theatre. Meyrink's grandfather was an unsuccessful actor; when his daughter Marie was born in 1841, he was described on the birth certificate as an 'out-of-work theatre cashier'. His wife, who came from Hengsberg, a village to the south of Graz in Austria, was a singer and much more successful; she became the family breadwinner, along with her eldest daughter, Marie Luise, who was to become one of Wagner's favourite singers. When the second daughter took up an engagement in Braunschweig, the family split up. Friedrich Meyer went to live with his brother and their youngest daughter Marie stayed with her mother, foreshadowing Meyrink's own childhood as the offspring of an actress single mother.

After the birth of her son, Marie Meyer left Stuttgart and was engaged at the court theatre in Munich, her contract starting on 1 April 1869. She was said to have been one of Ludwig II's favourite actresses, taking part in the 'private theatre performances attended only by the king and perhaps one or two special friends or the minion of the moment, who

[2] A copy is held in the *Meyrinkiana* in the Bavarian State Library.

would sit in the box immediately below the king's[3] leaving him with the sense of being alone in the theatre, of being able to enjoy the spectacle without feeling he was himself a spectacle for the audience.

Marie Meyer remained in Munich until 1880, when she went to Hamburg. From 1883–1885 she was at the Deutsches Landestheater in Prague, then in St Petersburg until 1891, when she joined the Lessingtheater in Berlin, her last engagement. She retired from the stage in 1902 and died in 1906.

There is almost no documentary evidence for Meyrink's childhood years, no surviving letters from his mother or father, no memories of friends or classmates. He was apparently initially looked after by his grandmother in Hamburg but by 1874 he had joined his mother in Munich and attended primary school there, then secondary school, the Wilhelmsgymnasium. From 1881–1883 he attended secondary school, the Johanneum, in Hamburg and then completed his schooling in Prague. When his mother moved on to St Petersburg, he remained in Prague, where he took a course in banking at the commercial college there. His school reports from Hamburg indicate that he was an outstanding scholar and top of the class in both of the years he was there: 'Gustav has again completed the year to our complete satisfaction through his excellent achievements and good behaviour.'

This contradicts his own later statement to his children, reported by Schmid Noerr, that his marks were always unsatisfactory and yet he had still made something of himself.[4] However, Schmid Noerr, a long-standing friend of Meyrink, suggests he took his school-leaving examination in Munich

[3] See Wilfrid Blunt: *The Dream King*, Harmondsworth, 1973, p. 173.
[4] Alfred Schmid Noerr: 'Erinnerungen an Gustav Meyrink', *Münchner Neueste Nachrichten*, 5.3.1933.

15

(he went on to Hamburg and finished in Prague) and describes the school there as a *Realgymnasium* (specialising in science and modern languages), whereas the Wilhelmsgymnasium was the oldest school in Munich and a well-known *humanistisches Gymnasium*, ie based on classical studies.

All of this demonstrates the care one must take in assessing the evidence for Meyrink's life. Both Meyrink himself and his friends and acquaintances are unreliable, though not necessarily always wrong. The same care must be taken in assessing descriptions of his childhood:

'His childhood was bleak, as was to be expected for an illegitimate child in those days';[5] 'an emotionally deprived childhood, lacking any parental love, had left a deep mark on his character';[6] 'his to all appearances unhappy childhood';[7] 'little is known of Meyrink's childhood, but it was presumably unhappy'.[8] Meyrink's own comment on Bavaria, where he spent most of his childhood, suggests it was more normal than is generally supposed: 'When, forty-five years ago, I was brought by the Pilot to this city [Prague] from foggy Hamburg, I was dazzled by a bright sun . . . a sun which seemed quite different from the cheerfully shining skies of bright, carefree Bavaria.'[9] Commentators, then, are unanimous in their conjecture that Meyrink's childhood was unhappy. But it remains a conjecture based on the few known

[5] Hans Arnold Plöhn: 'Zur achtzigsten Wiederkehr des Geburtstages Gustav Meyrinks am 19. Januar 1948', *Der Zwiebelfisch*, 1948/9, no. 8, pp. 7-9.

[6] Eduard Frank: *Gustav Meyrink. Werk und Wirkung*, Büdingen-Gettenbach, 1957, p. 10.

[7] Mohammad Qasim: *Gustav Meyrink. Eine monographische Untersuchung*, Stuttgart, 1981, p. 41.

[8] Karin Pircher: *'Ein Bürger zweier Welten'. Wiederkehrende Motive in den Romanen Gustav Meyrinks*, MA thesis, University of Innsbruck, 2005, p. 5.

[9] Gustav Meyrink: 'Die Stadt mit dem heimlichen Herzschlag' in: *Das Haus zur letzten Latern*, Frankfurt/M, Berlin, 1993, p. 157.

facts: his illegitimate birth; being an only child; having no father, and a working mother; changes of school because of his mother's engagements at different theatres (three after the birth of her son: Munich – Hamburg – Prague, though for some commentators that tends to become 'numerous'). That is the sum total of what is known. It doubtless influenced Meyrink's development, but there will have been other factors that are unknown.

His relationship with his mother

Much more space is taken up with discussions of Meyrink's relationship with his mother. Again, almost nothing is known of this. The one letter from his mother that has survived is a card with a few words in rather spidery writing and difficult to read in detail, but the tone seems warm and appropriate for a mother to her married 29-year-old son, ending as it does 'with most affectionate kisses . . . for you and Hedwig from your mother.' The fact that it is the only letter from his mother that was not thrown away or destroyed is not of significance. As mentioned above, the only letters Meyrink appears to have kept are either those dealing with matters of business or those connected with his interest in the occult. Qasim, talking of the occult and magic in Meyrink's writings says:

It is therefore quite natural that the mysterious quality of Meyrink's works should draw the reader's attention to the person of the author. Meyrink, however, seems to have been all too well aware of the reader's interest or, rather, curiosity about biographical details. He left behind very little to satisfy such curiosity or to allow one to construct a biography.

(Quasim, 33)

and goes on to quote from Meyrink's 'Description of myself', in which he talks about himself in the third person: 'Personal characteristics: he does not reply to personal letters, receives no visitors and does not visit people himself.'[10]

'Other people love their mothers, he hated her.'[11] Herbert Fritsche's lapidary assertion reflects the general assessment of Meyrink's relationship with his mother. Its basis is not so much documentary evidence as his portrayal of mothers in his novels. The only good mother seems to be a dead mother – Miriam's mother in *The Golem*, for example, perhaps Christopher's in *The White Dominican*, though she is a traditional Catholic and didn't understand her husband's 'spiritual path'.[12] In *Walpurgisnacht* Countess Zahradka shoots her illegitimate son Ottokar, who is being carried along as a figurehead by the revolutionary Czechs, with the words 'There you have your crown, bastard!'[13] Ophelia in *The White Dominican* confesses to Christopher, 'It is not for my mother's sake that I am asking you not to do it . . . I don't love her. I can't help it, I'm ashamed of her.' More significantly, perhaps, Ophelia's mother is an actress and wants to put her daughter on the stage, an idea which Ophelia finds repugnant:

> It seems to me repulsive and ugly to stand up in front of people and act out delight or mental torment before them . . . And to do that evening after evening, and always at the same time! I feel that I am being asked to prostitute my soul.
>
> (*Dominican*, 76)

---

[10] *Meyrinkiana*; also printed in *Der Zwiebelfisch*, 1925, p. 26.

[11] Quoted in Frank, p. 19.

[12] Gustav Meyrink: *The White Dominican*, tr. Mike Mitchell, Sawtry/ Riverside, 1994, p. 100.

[13] Gustav Meyrink: *Walpurgisnacht*, tr. Mike Mitchell, Sawtry/ Riverside, 1993, p. 167.

It is a strong condemnation of his own mother's profession, even if put into the mouth of a fictional character. However, we must also bear in mind that this was written fifteen years after his mother's death and in between he had made several not very successful attempts to establish himself, together with a writer called Roda Roda, as a dramatist. It seems flimsy evidence for his feelings towards his mother as a child. Counter evidence could be seen in the comment by the hero of *The White Dominican* on his mother: '. . . my first name of Christopher . . . It is the only thing I have from her and that is why I have always regarded the name of Christopher as something sacred.' (*Dominican*, 19)

The key text in discussions of Meyrink's feelings about his mother is a long short story called 'The Master', first published in the collection *Fledermäuse* (Bats) in 1916.[14] The Swiss writer Max Pulver wrote about Meyrink in his memoirs:

In all the years of our acquaintance he never spoke of his mother . . . Naturally I never asked about his parents, but once, he might have been asking about *my* background, he suddenly gave a clue to the woman. She is portrayed in his story "The Master". He did not go on, did not add anything to that.[15]

How much credence we can give to this it is difficult to say. Pulver was over 20 years younger than Meyrink; his father died when he was seven and, according to his biography, 'his relations with his mother remained difficult throughout his life.'[16] Was he projecting his own problems onto Meyrink?

---

[14] 'The Master' in: *The Dedalus Book of Austrian Fantasy 1890–2000*, ed. & tr. Mike Mitchell, Sawtry 2003.

[15] Max Pulver: *Erinnerungen an eine europäische Zeit*, Zurich, 1953, pp. 72-3.

[16] 'Pulver' in: Internet 'project gutenberg'.

Some of the 'facts' he quotes are incorrect, for example he makes the, admittedly often repeated, mistake of confusing Meyrink's mother Marie Meyer with 'a famous Jewish actress' Clara Meyer and spells the name 'Meier', which looks more 'Jewish'.

However, the portrait of the mother in 'The Master' is certainly striking. The hard-hearted mothers in *Walpurgisnacht* and *The White Dominican* can be explained by their function in the novels, but that is not the case with Leonhard's mother in 'The Master'. The first twenty pages of this 46-page story contain a vitriolic portrait of a mother seen through her son's memories for which there is no real narrative necessity, certainly not for the extreme vehemence of Leonhard's feeling. The story does appear to be, at least in part, a vehicle for the outpouring of hatred. For example:

> Once again he feels the bitter hatred of his mother rising in his gorge . . . A wish that his mother might be found dead in her bed one morning quietly surfaces inside him . . . Leonhard . . . is already as tall as his mother. When he stands facing her, his eyes are on the same level as hers, but he always feels compelled to look away, not daring to give way to the constant prick of the urge to fix her vacant stare and pour into it all the searing hatred he feels for her . . . A spurt of dread paralyses Leonhard. He stares at her, horrified, as if she were a creature he were looking at for the first time. There is nothing human about her any longer, she appears to him as an alien being from some hell, half goblin, half vicious animal.
>
> (*Austrian Fantasy*, 39, 41, 44)

Leonhard murders his mother by letting a trapdoor fall on her head when she observes him making love to Sabina (his sister, though at the time they do not know it) in the chapel of

Marie Meyer, his mother, in costume

the family castle. The crowding together into this one incident of incest, desecration and matricide, together with the physical intensity of the setting and event – nakedness, physical violence, the Gothic architecture, the figure of the mother rising from the vault to observe her son and daughter in the act of coition, the splintering crash as the trapdoor falls on her head – could suggest it had its origin in some deep psychological need.

It is, however, still extremely uncertain how far these figures can be interpreted biographically. Some female characters in Meyrink's novels do have a part in the spiritual life, but their role tends to be passive rather than active (Lizzie the Czech in *Walpurgisnacht* may be considered an exception); their spirituality is part of what they *are*, rather than coming from what they do, from following what Christopher's father calls his 'spiritual path'. They are adjuncts, if in some ways superior, to the male heroes and they frequently die (Miriam, Ophelia, Eva in *The Green Face*) before any physical union is achieved – to be brought together in a perfect, almost hermaphroditic union after death. It fits in with this structure for female figures who remain in the world and active in the hero's life to be negatively charged, to be part of the force dragging him down, hampering his spiritual growth. Leonhard's final thoughts on his mother fit in just as well with this than as reflections of Meyrink's hatred of his own mother:

> He is tormented by concern for Sabina. He knows this is the earthenward pull of his mother's curse-laden blood in his veins trying to curb his soaring flight, trying to smother the youthful fire of his enthusiasms with the grey ashes of mundane reality . . .
>
> (*Austrian Fantasy*, 57)

2

Prague

Meyrink went to Prague in 1883 and lived there until 1904, that is, from the age of 15 to 36. The middle to later teens are very important for a person's *intellectual* development and Prague certainly left its stamp on Meyrink. After Prague he lived for a short while in Vienna, briefly in Montreux then spent his last twenty-six years in Bavaria. As far as his writing and his interest in the occult was concerned, however, it was his years in Prague that were the decisive influence on his outlook.

The Prague that Meyrink came to in 1883 was a city in transition. Writing in 1913, James Baker, who had been travelling to the Austro-Hungarian Empire since 1873, said: 'I remember Prague when it was apparently a wholly German city; today the traveller will quickly see that it is a Slav city, but the Germans, although only about 6 per cent. of the population, have their theatre and schools, and the historic university.'[1] In 1850 German-speakers made up half the city's population and were dominant socially, culturally and politically. By 1880 the higher Czech birth-rate, the migration of workers from the countryside and the incorporation of outlying districts mainly inhabited by Czechs had reduced this to 14% and by 1910 to 6–7%. In the middle of the 19th century there was still a sense of Germans and Czechs

[1] James Baker: *Austria: her People & their Homelands*, illus. Donald Maxwell, London, 1913, p. 26.

belonging to the same community, of peaceful cooperation within Bohemia (*Čechy* = Bohemia), of collaboration against Viennese centralism.

By the 1880s this 'Bohemianism' was fast disappearing under the onslaught of increasingly virulent nationalism – and anti-Semitism, around 45% of the German-speaking population was Jewish. This loss of a 'Bohemian' community was something Rilke, who was born in Prague, deeply regretted. His early volume of poems, *Larenopfer* (Offering to the Household Gods, 1895) is a celebration of Prague and Bohemia, 'a Bohemia which seems to belong half to the past, half to a utopian future . . . and is no less fictitious than Shakespeare's Bohemia by the sea.'[2] The uncertainty about identity this created, especially among the Jewish community, has been well documented in the life of Kafka.

For the Czechs on the other hand, who had fully taken over the city council by 1888, Prague was to become the symbol of the resurgent nation. That meant industrialisation, slum clearance and redevelopment, including the razing of the Josefstadt, the old Jewish quarter, apart from the cemetery, town hall and some of the older synagogues. As James Baker wrote just before the First World War:

> This famous old city, with a tremendous history, *Zlata Praha*, Golden Prague, as the Slavs so love to call it, is being, or rather has been, transformed during the last twenty years. The crooked, nauseous, dirty streets through which one twisted and wandered thirty years ago have nearly all disappeared.
>
> (Baker, 21)

---

[2] Commentary on Rilke: *Gedichte 1895–1910*, ed. Manfred Engel, Ulrich Fülleborn, Frankfurt/M., Leipzig, 1996, p. 632.

For the declining German population, to which Meyrink belonged, and especially for the writers and artists, Prague became associated with the past, with decay, an image both gloomy and romantic. A prime example is the art of Hugo Steiner, who added 'Prag' to his name and was later to illustrate Meyrink's *Golem*. Despite its wealth of ancient monuments, what raises Prague above other cities of similar age is not so much the quality of the architecture as such as the atmosphere it creates as a whole, from the heights of Hradčany, looming over the alleys of the *Malá Strana*, the lesser town on the left bank, to the Jewish ghetto, the old town square and the spiky towers of the Tyn Church across the river. It was an atmosphere that left its mark on Meyrink who called it 'The City with the Secret Heartbeat':

The city I am talking about is old *Prague* . . . Even then, forty-five years ago, as I walked over the ancient Stone Bridge which crosses the calm waters of the Moldau to Hradčany, the hill with its dark castle exuding the arrogance of ancient generations of Habsburgs, I was overcome with a profound sense of horror, for which I could find no explanation. Since that day this feeling of apprehension has never left me for a moment during all the time – the length of a whole generation – I lived in Prague, the city with the secret heartbeat. It has never entirely left me, even today it comes over me when I think back to Prague or dream of it at night. Everything I ever experienced I can call up in my mind's eye as if it were there before me, bursting with life. If, however, I summon up Prague, it appears more clearly than anything else, so clearly, in fact, that it no longer seems real, but ghostly. Every person I knew there turns into a ghost, an inhabitant of a realm that does not know death.

Puppets do not die when they leave the stage; and all

the beings the city with the secret heartbeat holds together are puppets. Other cities, however old they may be, seem to me to be under the power of their people; as if disinfected by germicidal acids, Prague shapes and manipulates its inhabitants like a puppeteer from their first to their last breath. Just as volcanoes spew forth fire out of the earth, so this eerie city spews war and revolution out into the world . . .

(Latern, 157–8)

Prague and his experiences there were the most significant formative influence on Meyrink both as a writer and for his interest in the occult. He left the city after a very public scandal and a period of imprisonment awaiting trial had contributed to the ruin of both his business and his health. For some time afterwards his feelings for the city turned to hatred, which he expressed for example in the story 'G.M.', first published in 1904, shortly after he had left Prague. The hero, George Mackintosh, leaves a 'grand visiting card' behind him in a town that is unnamed but clearly Prague.[3] What this is becomes apparent when a photographer takes a picture of the town from the balloon Mackintosh has left: the rumour of buried gold he spread has caused the citizens to demolish houses so that they form the initials G M when seen from the air.[4]

Despite this, Prague remained with Meyrink for the rest of his life. It was to become the setting for his novels *The Golem, Walpurgisnacht*, and, in part, *The Angel of the West Window*. He also came to see it more positively, as in the essay 'The City with the Secret Heartbeat' quoted from above. It was not

---

[3] Like Prague, it has a Ferdinand Street, a Joseph Square.

[4] In: Gustav Meyrink: *The Opal*, tr. and intro. Maurice Raraty, Sawtry, 1994, pp. 206–213.

merely the setting for his interest in the occult, it partook of the occult itself.

If Prague influenced Meyrink, Meyrink influenced the image of Prague in the wider world. He was one of the key figures in the creation of the myth of 'magic Prague', which in the 1960s 'was seized upon by the dissident left, both in Prague and elsewhere, in protest against the decaying prescriptions of socialist realism'[5] and today has somewhat degenerated into a romantic image used to attract the tourist trade.

The Banker

Meyrink finished his schooling in Prague, then attended the commercial college there. He appears to have managed to avoid military service. In the archives is his *Landsturmschein*, a certificate attesting his membership of the militia that was only called up in emergency. A note explains that he was assigned to the *Landsturm*, instead of being sent to join the regular army, because 'after he had reported for military service he had been rejected by the King's Own Regiment in Munich as mentally unsuitable'. Lube points out that this condition can hardly have been genuine, quoting Meyrink's son-in-law's suspicion that Meyrink managed to fool the recruiting board.[6]

On completion of his studies, he worked as a banker. This area of his life is as mystifying as anything else in it. There is virtually no documentary evidence to provide dates and details. The majority version is that he set up a bank, Meyer & Morgenstern, with a nephew of the well-known German

---

[5] Peter Demetz: *Prague in Black and Gold*, New York, 1997, pp. xiii–xiv.

[6] Manfred Lube: *Gustav Meyrink. Beiträge zur Biographie und Studien zu seiner Kunsttheorie,* Graz, 1980, p. 191.

writer of philosophical nonsense verse, Christian Morgenstern. Schmid Noerr says he '*joined* the bank of Morgenstern
at the age of twenty,'[7] but Schmid Noerr, as we have seen, can
be inaccurate and is not always to be trusted on details, despite
his close relationship with Meyrink in the 1920s. The date at
which the Meyer & Morgenstern bank was established is
variously given as 1888 and 1889; Gerhard Böttcher says 'he
joined an export house as a trainee in 1888 and founded the
bank of Meyer & Morgenstern the following year.'[8] The most
convincing account is that outlined by Mohammed Qasim
(42–3), where he points out that when he reached maturity –
in 1889 – Meyrink received the large sum of money his father
had deposited for him, the interest from which had until then
been paid to his mother to finance his upbringing. A contemporary assessment puts the amount at 18,250 marks.[9] The
assumption is that he used this money, or part of it, as his
investment in the joint bank. Later he broke up with Morgenstern and set up on his own, allegedly describing his business
as 'the first Christian bank in Prague'. (quoted in Lube, 218)
No date for this has been established. Manfred Lube (11)
points out that letters to Meyrink between 1893 and 1897 are
addressed to the bank at 33 Wenceslas Square, while he later
used a letter heading: Bankgeschäft Gustav Meyer (Gustav
Meyer's Bank), 59 Brenntegasse, but no precise date for the
change has been found, nor how it was connected with his

[7] Alfred Schmid Noerr: afterword to Gustav Meyrink: *Des deutschen
Spießers Wunderhorn*, p. 185.

[8] Gerhard Böttcher: afterword to *Des deutschen Spießers Wunderhorn* Berlin,
1969, p. 274.

[9] Giving the current equivalent in pounds for a sum in marks in 1890 is
difficult. A straightforward currency conversion via Euros suggests a sum of
over £200,000. Other calculations based on cost of living, average earnings,
GDP etc. put it somewhat lower or a lot higher. Whatever the precise figure,
Meyrink certainly had a considerable sum of money at his disposal.

break with Morgenstern. Many articles, especially those following his death in 1932, suggest he was cheated out of his
inheritance by his partner,[10] but his second wife insisted there
was no truth in that and the collapse of his bank was entirely
due to his own incompetence in financial matters.

Lube also points out that the business is sometimes referred
to as a *Bankgeschäft* (banking house), sometimes as a more
lowly *Wechselstube* (bureau de change), both by Meyrink himself and in official documents. In the autobiographical text
'Die Verwandlung des Blutes' (The Transformation of the
Blood) Meyrink describes himself as 'owner of a bureau de
change', but on the next page says he was visited by a man
who had been sent to see 'a banker called M';[11] his Alpine
Club membership card calls him a 'banker', an official document of 1901 calls him 'owner of a bureau de change', while
one from 1906 calls him a 'former banker in Prague'. His
business was ruined in 1902 by a false accusation of fraud. As
he was accused of misappropriating clients' money and stocks
and shares, it seems likely that his business was more than just a
bureau de change; a newspaper article on him says that he 'was
a banker in Prag, they called it *Wechselherr* there,'[12] suggesting
the two terms were interchangeable.

The Dandy

Despite the fact that he remained a banker until 1902, all the
testimony of his friends and acquaintances, even that of his

[10] For example Viktor Schweizer: 'Der Bürgerschreck von Prag' in the
Hannoversches Tageblatt of 7.12.32 and Gustaf Kauder: 'Meyrink gestorben'
in the *Berliner Zeitung* of 5.12.32.

[11] Gustav Meyrink: 'Die Verwandlung des Blutes' in *Fledermäuse*, ed. Eduard
Frank, Frankfurt/M & Berlin, 1992, pp. 221 & 224.

[12] *Münchener Kultur-Pressedienst* 3.8.46.

second wife, suggests he was temperamentally unsuited to the profession. Roda Roda described him as 'unbelievably naive in financial matters'[13] and his wife, in a letter to William van Buskirk, said 'My husband was a hopeless businessman and ruined the banking business.'

Indeed, once he had come into his inheritance, he embarked on an extravagant lifestyle completely at odds with the respectable image of a banker:

> He bought loud ties and extravagant suits, the most ultramodern shoes available in Prague in the 1890s. He bought overbred dogs, a whole cageful of white mice, a whole pack of exotic pets . . . All done with the conscious intention of provoking all the respectable, all-too respectable people of the city, of arousing their animosity.[14]

and

> He took part in fencing bouts in the Gentlemen's Club until two or three in the morning, was a member of the Prague Casino and attended countless exclusive parties. Once he rode right through Prague on a horse drawing a carriage with singers and actors waving coloured balloons.[15]

It seems almost inevitable that he was one of the first people, at least as he claimed, to own a motor car in Prague. Schweizer, in the article following his death quoted above, says he was the 'first agent for these newly invented vehicles' there.

[13] Roda Roda in: *Vossische Zeitung* no. 340, 1933.

[14] Schweizer, loc. cit.

[15] Strelka, 7.

Meyrink as a young man

A more elaborate 'Meyrink story' is told by the writer Fritz von Herzmanovsky-Orlando. Meyrink used to travel regularly on business to Dresden. His frequent trips, his arrogant looks and his elegant luggage aroused the suspicions of the border officials and the border checks became more and more exhaustive. After he had put up with this for long enough, he devised a way of getting his own back on the customs officials. He had a steel insert fitted to his small suitcase allowing him to force a large number of damp towels in under hydraulic pressure:

When the train stopped at the border the customs officer appeared and put the usual question: 'Anything to declare?'

Meyrink, also as usual, replied 'No' from behind his newspaper.

The official's eye was caught by the new and extremely elegant leather case. It was a good inch larger than the permitted size, as he immediately noted with disapproval.

'What's in there?'

'Washing.'

'What kind of washing?'

'Just a few towels for my personal use. I've been in Lahmann's Sanatorium.'

'Towels? A whole case full? Open it.'

Meyrink replied in polite tones that as a result of the hurried departure, the towels had been slightly damp when packed and it might be difficult to close the case again afterwards. As an officer of the reserve he gave his word of honour that the washing –'

'Sorry,' the official broke in, 'would you be so good as to get the case down.'

Meyrink shrugged his shoulders. 'I can't. It's too heavy for me.'

The official, visibly irritated, grasped the case himself and gasped. The improbable weight of the small piece of luggage only sent his suspicions soaring. And, as a groping inspection revealed, it was padlocked into the bargain! He looked the increasingly suspect passenger up and down with the gimlet stare taught on courses for examining magistrates and similar officials, then had the offending piece of luggage dragged into the customs hall by two porters, escorting Meyrink there himself.

A senior official in his spinach-coloured uniform was brought from his glass cabin. Annoyed at being disturbed in his reading, he folded his arms and gave Meyrink, who stood there with an air of injured innocence, a long, hard stare. Then he tapped the suitcase with his finger and asked haughtily, 'And what have we here?'

Meyrink repeated his explanation, obligingly handing over the keys but adding that if they opened the case it would be on their own responsibility. He was on important business, had to be in Prague by three for a meeting with some VIPs in the world of finance and didn't want to cause a delay, from which he would be the one to suffer most. He repeated his warning that they wouldn't be able to get the towels back in the suitcase and they wouldn't expect him to continue his journey with an armful of damp towels, would they? Especially as he'd been telling the pure unvarnished truth.

'We'll see about that,' replied the official scornfully. 'Seems a bit heavy for washing, if you ask me. Perhaps the knights of old had washing like that when they went on the Crusades, but you can't fool me, sir. I know what's in there. Precious metal, that's what it is. Stojesbal, take the keys and open that thing.'

Scarcely had the customs officer opened one of the locks than the other came off automatically, the case sprang open and an endless stream of towels poured out with a quiet humming noise. The senior official and his minions threw themselves on the mysterious suitcase, trying to push the lid down. In vain. The hydraulic mechanism was stronger.

Half an hour later Meyrink, flanked by two baskets that had been hurriedly found, the contents of which were still softly humming, was steaming towards the capital.

From then on the customs officials left him in peace.[16]

As Eduard Frank reports, he could also deal with a phoney prophet with the same impish humour:

A 'miracle-working apostle' called Häuser woke him up one night with his knocking and constant cries of 'I am'. When Meyrink politely enquired who he was, he replied, 'I am Christ.' Meyrink immediately opened the door, took his visitor to the side of the lake and said, gesturing towards the water, 'Then walk, please.' At that the miracle-worker dropped his pretence and said in a pitiful voice, 'I'm hungry.' Meyrink invited the unmasked saint in to have breakfast.

(Frank, 15)

And it was not only his dress and behaviour that was extravagant, his apartment, too, lived up to its owner's outrageous appearance:

He had a terrarium with two African mice he had given

---

[16] Fritz von Herzmanovsky-Orlando: *Maskenspiel der Genien. Romane und Erzählungen*, Munich/ Vienna, 1971, pp. 259–261.

the names of characters from Maeterlinck, a genuine confessional he had dug up God knows where, pictures of Madame Blavatsky, the sculpture of a ghost disappearing into the wall and lots of other things that had no place in the home of a banker.[17]

Paul Leppin, who wrote this description, was one of the circle of young people, many of them writers and artists, who gathered round Meyrink. Leppin was a writer and modelled the mysterious figure of Herr Nikolaus in his novel *Severin's Road to Darkness* on Meyrink. Indeed, the description of Nikolaus's apartment is very close to that of Meyrink's quoted above.[18] Like Meyrink, Leppin's character is also a slightly older figure who has an air of mystery about him, is in some ways aloof, reserved about his personal background, yet also the centre of attention; in brief, he has what we would nowadays call charisma. There was a rumour that Meyrink was of royal descent, perhaps the illegitimate son of King Ludwig II of Bavaria, which he seems to have done nothing to discourage.

Meyrink's notoriety was such that Thomas Mann used him, without mentioning his name, in his novella of 1903, *Tonio Kröger*, as a figure embodying two contradictory qualities, the respectability of the bourgeois and the dubious nature of the artist:

I know a banker, a grey-haired businessman, who has a talent for writing short stories. He exercises this talent in his leisure hours. Despite – I say 'despite' – this admirable ability, this man's reputation is not entirely spotless.

[17] Paul Leppin: 'Bankier Meyer. Erinnerungen an Gustav Meyrinks Prager Zeit', *Zeit im Bild*, 1932, no 8, pp. 4–5.

[18] Paul Leppin *The Roàd to Darkness*, tr. Mike Mitchell, Sawtry & Riverside, 1997, p. 86.

On the contrary, he was condemned to a lengthy prison
sentence, and for good reason. Indeed, it was actually in
prison that he first became aware of his talent . . . One
could, then, make the somewhat bold deduction that
one must first be at home in some kind of penal institution in order to become a writer, an artist.[19]

By his own later admission, he was determined to become
the 'vainest, most systematic dandy of Prague'.[20] The deliberate courting of notoriety was presumably a response to his
equivocal position. He was wealthy, but he was also an outsider. And he was illegitimate. When this fact became public
knowledge is not certain, perhaps from the very beginning,
while his mother was still in Prague, but it was used later in
the 1890s by officers he had challenged as an excuse not to
fight him, to declare his illegitimacy rendered him 'incapable
of giving satisfaction'.

The obverse of the deliberate pose was a certain introver-
sion. It is perhaps significant that the group he became closest
to in the later 1890s consisted of younger men, who looked
up to him. Hugo Steiner-Prag, the artist who was later to
illustrate *Der Golem*, described their response to him:

They were remarkable years for us, a small group of
close friends, young artists and writers, a tightly knit
community which you unexpectedly joined one day.
We looked on you in amazement, much older than we
were and in your outward appearance so at odds with
our rather informal and exuberant Bohemianism. At

[19] Thomas Mann: 'Tonio Kröger', in *Frühe Erzählungen 1893–1912*, Frank-
furt/M, 2004, pp. 73–4. As we will see later, Meyrink was merely
imprisoned awaiting trial and released without charge.
[20] F. A. Schmid Noerr: 'Erinnerungen an G. M.' in a supplement to *Münchner Neueste Nachrichten* 5.3.33.

first we had no idea what brought you, Herr Meyer the banker, well-known in society, the elegant sportsman, to our little circle.[21]

He was in fact only twelve years older than Steiner-Prag. Appearing older than he was, was perhaps part of the protect- ive shell he had grown. The initial impression he made on Max Brod, who was sixteen years his junior, was of 'a middle- aged man . . . at least twenty, perhaps thirty years older than us . . . He looked like an extremely elegant, slim, slightly ailing retired officer.'[22]

Besides an audience for his fantastic anecdotes, for which he was well-known even before he started writing, and his caustic mockery of establishment society, such a group gave him gregariousness without intimacy, allowing him to keep his innermost self undisclosed. This was most clearly expressed in his eyes. They were large and lustrous and often seemed to be looking past those around him, into some depths beyond the everyday world. Max Pulver describes meeting him in 1916: 'A slim man in his forties, with a wiry elegance, a long skull that seemed almost bald and deep-set eyes that pene- trated the depths.'[23] This expressiveness can still be felt even today in photographs of him. Max Brod continues his descrip- tion of his first sight of Meyrink by emphasising the outsider who gave the impression of being *above* the crowd milling around him:

He could be seen taking his stroll along the Graben [Na Příkopě] every Sunday morning; he was always alone, one leg limping a little . . . His expression was arrogant,

[21] Hugo Steiner-Prag: preface to 1931 edition of *Der Golem*, pp. 6–7; (quoted in Strelka, p. 7).
[22] Max Brod: *Streitbares Leben*, Munich, 1960, p. 292.
[23] Pulver, p. 37.

reserved. Occasionally a scornful gleam would appear in his large blue eyes. He always kept to the extreme edge of the pavement, as if he had to have a clear view of the whole swarm of passers-by, as if he must not let one of them out of his sight . . . I watched him from a distance with a shudder of reverence.[24]

To add to the contradiction of the banker and the dandy, Meyrink was also a keen and outstanding sportsman. He had a reputation as an excellent fencer – the real reason, it is some-times implied, why the officers refused his challenge – but rowing was his greatest interest, an interest that amounted to a passion. The rowing magazine *Der Rudersport* of 2 August 1916 gives details of his successes: 'Meyrink has a successful career in rowing behind him . . . He competed in regattas in Budapest, Dresden, Leitmeritz, Pirna, Prague, Raudnitz and Vienna, as well as in Switzerland, and had 32 victories from 67 starts. In 1887 he won the German-Bohemian Champion-ship in Leitmeritz and in 1888 the Championship on the Moldau in Prague.'[25] His charismatic appeal to other, espe-cially younger people, which he exerted over the writers and artists in Prague, also clearly extended to athletes. *Der Rudersport* reported in 1913 that:

the Bayern Rowing Club has entrusted the training of its rowers to the well-known writer, Gustav Meyrink; with his experience of racing he has the necessary prac-tical knowledge and he knows how to strike the right tone in his dealings with the crews, so that they have become very attached to him.[26]

[24] Max Brod, loc. cit.
[25] Quoted in Dirk Heisserer: *Wellen Wind und Dorfbanditen. Literarische Erkundungen am Starnberger See*, Munich, 1995, pp. 32–3.
[26] Ibid.

He went about his rowing with the same intensity almost amounting to obsession with which he pursued other interests which were close to his heart. He told a journalist who visited him in 1931 that he was still doing eight hours of yoga practice every day and four hours rowing.[27] At least for the latter there is some documentary evidence: *Rudersport* (12.2.1916) reported that he went out almost daily adding, mischievously, 'and who knows, perhaps *The Golem* was partly thought out in his single scull.' (Heisserer, 34) When the Rowing Club congratulated their distinguished member on the success of *The Golem* and *The Green Face*, they added that Meyrink 'could also have claimed the 1916 prize for the most kilometres and the most outings, since he did long distances almost every day.' (Heisserer, 35) When Max Brod visited him in his house on Lake Starnberg 'a good time after *The Golem* was published' (1915), Meyrink told him he spent 'hours training in his rowing boat, the lake was ideal for that sport.'[28] To Francis in 1931 he claimed he was still the rowing champion of the veteran class of German Bohemia – though without saying when he actually won the championship.

His continued attachment to rowing was despite a serious illness he suffered from the late 1890s to the early 1900s. The illustrator, Thomas Theodor Heine, reported:

> He used to tell of strange things . . . He could, he said, leave his body at will. He showed me a snapshot of himself in his single scull winning the great race on the Thames.
>
> 'And do you know who took the photo? I did. I left my body and mingled with the onlookers with my camera.'

[27] Francis: *Hannoverscher Anzeiger* 18.10.31.
[28] Brod, p. 305.

Meyrink in his single scull on Lake Starnberg

He claimed he had sent the photo to his Prague doctors who had diagnosed an incurable disease of the spine only one year previously.[29]

Although one tends to take this story with a large pinch of salt, he had obviously resumed his rowing as soon as he could after recovering from the illness; nor did the slight limp it left him with stop him climbing mountains again – at least he claims to have fallen 1,000 feet down the Dent de Jaman, presumably in 1905–6 when he was living in nearby Montreux.

It was this contradiction between the athletic sportsman and the famed writer of occult novels that Josef Schneiderfranken, himself a popular mystic who wrote under the name of Bô Yin Râ, emphasised in 1921:

anyone who sees him in his scull, parting the waves with powerful strokes, would hardly think that this sinewy, supple rower is the author of *The Golem*, whom one would rather imagine, like his hero Athanasius Pernath, in a little room high up in the Prague ghetto, as far as possible from the open air.[30]

As we will see later, physical activity and interest in the occult were not mutually exclusive; in fact they combined in the yoga exercises he practised throughout his life.

Two Marriages

Meyrink got married on 1 March 1893. Some writers, for example Eduard Frank, give 1892, but a letter from an

---

[29] Thomas Theodor Heine: *Münchner Sonntags-Anzeiger* no. 50.

[30] Josef Schneiderfranken: 'Der Dichter des *Golem*', *Magische Blätter*, 1921; reprinted in *Fledermäuse*, p. 390.

astrologer to Meyrink says: 'According to what you have told me . . . your marriage of 1 March 1893 has so far remained childless.' His first wife was Hedwig Aloysia Certl. Nothing appears to be known about her or how they met. It is clear, however, that the marriage very quickly turned out to be a mistake. The only mention of her in his writings is in the essay 'Haschisch und Hellsehen' (Hashish and Clairvoyance). Meyrink had decided to experiment with drugs, under the supervision of a doctor friend. In the middle of the experiment, his first wife came into the room:

> From the beginning she had been very afraid the experiment with hashish could damage my health and had therefore been violently opposed to it from the start. A pretty vehement argument developed between her and my doctor friend, which ended with her abruptly leaving the room and slamming the door behind her.
>
> (*Latern*, 254)

Perhaps the best evidence we have for their relationship is a picture of the couple. The spark, which is discernible in almost all other photographs of Meyrink, is completely absent. His eyes are dull, his expression wooden, his clothes lack the extravagance of the 'vainest, most systematic dandy in Prague'. Perhaps his first wife wanted to make him become the respectable banker that he seemed determined to avoid being? They certainly appear to have been ill-suited.

It was in 1897 that he met and fell in love with Mena (real name Philomena) Bernt, the woman who was to become his second wife. That is the year as noted by Meyrink on the horoscope from the astrologer mentioned above and it also occurs in a letter from Mena Meyrink herself to Buskirk, who in spite of that gives the year as 1896. The attraction was mutual, despite someone sitting next to Mena warning her against him: 'Don't have anything to do with him – he's a

Meyrink with his first wife

black magician.'[31] The effect, Meyrink's second wife maintained, was draw her attention to him. They soon got secretly engaged, but had to wait a further seven years before they could marry, since Meyrink's first wife refused a divorce. When a mutual friend persuaded her to change her mind, they travelled to England, to avoid scandal, and were married in the Congregational Church, High St, Dover on 8 May 1905. It was a happy marriage, they seem to have been genuine soulmates; Eduard Frank (11–12) calls Mena Meyrink her husband's 'guardian angel'.

[31] William R. van Buskirk: *The Bases of Satire in the Works of Gustav Meyrink*, PhD thesis, Michigan, 1957, p. 16.

3

The Occult

It was during the years in Prague that what we might conveniently call 'the occult' started to assume the central role it was later to play in Meyrink's life. Josef Strelka, while not denying his genuine interest, claims he deliberately contributed to the creation of the image of a man with supernatural powers:

> No German-language author of this [the 20th] century has attracted to his person such a multitude of legendary and invented, genuine and exaggerated ghost stories as Gustav Meyrink. And he himself encouraged this tendency through both his life and his books. It was not for nothing that, after time spent in Switzerland, England and Scotland, he built the house by Lake Starnberg which he called 'The House by the Last Lamp', recalling a ghostly building in Goldmakers Alley in Prague which is said to appear only to some people on certain nights and to be the threshold between two worlds.[1]

As the picture of Madame Blavatsky and the sculpture of a ghost going through the wall in his apartment attest, in his early years the occult provided some of the fashionable trappings of the dandy. For Max Brod the 'combination of the fourth dimension with the elegance of the dandy' was one of

[1] Strelka, pp. 9–10.

the most striking characteristics about Meyrink.[2] He provided
the hashish which was smoked by the small circle of friends,
experiments with table-rapping were carried out, seances
with mediums attended. There are numerous stories told by
his friends and by Meyrink himself about examples of magic
or clairvoyance.

He even, he claimed in 'Magie und Hasard' (Magic and
Chance), resorted to magic in an attempt to win at poker. He
found two methods which were supposed to influence chance
in one's favour. One was to fast and go on a 'diet' of castor oil,
the other was to tie a string tightly above the knee of one's left
leg until the lower half went numb. The latter seeming less
unpleasant, he decided to tie his handkerchief round his left
leg before joining in a poker game. He had awful cards. He
went out and tied a wet towel round his leg. His cards were
even worse, not even a pair. However, as he felt his leg go
completely numb, his luck seemed to change, he had a straight
flush to the queen. Everyone seemed to have good cards and
the betting rose astronomically. Eventually only Meyrink and
one other were left. His opponent, of course, had a flush to the
king. In the coffee house afterwards he discovered that his
opponent was using the castor-oil technique. Meyrink gave
up gambling, but when he met the other poker-player again
years later he discovered he hadn't made a fortune gambling,
but lost every last penny. He had never, he explained, managed to overcome either his addiction to gambling or his
dislike of castor oil. (*Latern*, 245–6)

One of the component parts of Meyrink's notoriety during his Prague years was the rumour that he was an alchemist
and trying to make gold, a rumour which he confirmed in an
article entitled 'How I Tried to Make Gold in Prague'. 'It
must have been about 1893, when I was still young and had

[2] Brod, p. 303.

plenty of time and leisure to do all the stupid things, the memory of which now brightens up my old age, that I decided to take up alchemy.' (*Latern*, 293)

The impulse to attempt practical alchemy came, he said, from a school-friend whose father had a glassworks. This friend told him an old chemist called Kinski, who worked there, added a light grey powder to ordinary glass to turn it into ruby glass, which was usually made with the addition of pure gold. (*Britannica* says gold chloride.) Kinski refused to divulge the secret of the powder. The only clues were his constant refrain of 'Gold is shit' and that he muttered something about a change of colour in the base matter.

Meyrink sought for the 'base matter' in his extensive alchemical library, but found nothing until one day a bookseller sent a book written by Count Marsciano:

> I leafed through it and all at once I knew – yes, I *knew* – what the base matter was: human or animal excrement! Shit, as old Kinski so aptly put it. The following sentence, however, only served to confuse me again: 'Our *materia* is yellow like butter, has a heavenly smell and tastes sweet as manna.' Furious, I threw the book in a corner . . . When I picked it up again, I saw that it was incomplete; the second part was missing. I wrote to all the antiquarian booksellers I could think of. In vain, no one had heard of it. Then an incredible coincidence intervened. I came across the catalogue of a book auction in Milan. Mechanically I opened it and saw: *Onuphrius Marsciano, volume two*. I immediately sent a telegram to Milan: Buy whatever the price. A few days later I had the little jewel in my hand and devoured it as the whale did Jonah. Strangely enough, the ex libris was the same as in the first volume I had . . . Had I been superstitious, I could almost have believed old Kinski had had a hand in it.

The second volume of Marsciano's work reveals that excrement that has been under the ground for a long time sometimes turns into the matter described in the first volume. Meyrink made enquiries of chemists as to whether that was possible, with no result, apart from a challenge from a chemistry student who belonged to a duelling fraternity. However, chance intervened once more:

One night I was going home late from a rowing-club party, dressed in white flannels and blue blazer, my athlete's chest decorated with countless medals won at regattas glittering in the moonlight. The main street in Prague had been dug up and a terrible miasma was floating up from the bowels of Mother Earth, for ancient sewers were being torn from their age-old sleep. Galvanised by this opportunity, I climbed a wall and shouted down into the yawning depths, 'Ahoy!' The flip-flop noise of a pump was replaced with deathly silence and soon the king of the night appeared from the abyss, a little lamp on his forehead, like some deep-sea fish. I stuck a twenty-crown note on the ferrule of my walking stick and thus passed it to the king. The following dialogue then took place:

Me: 'Your Pungency, have you, in the field of your endeavours, ever come across matter which is yellow as butter, fragrant and sweet to the taste?'

King of the Night: 'Not matter, no, but shit, yes. But only very rarely. A curiosity. If you look out for it you can find some. I know what you're after, of course, squire. They say it brings luck.'

Me: Excellent! Bring me some, my dear sir, as soon and as much as you can and you will be handsomely rewarded.'

Months passed. Summer had spread its fragrance over the city, for that was before there were motor cars. I was

The young Meyrink with his rowing medals

in my office entertaining some elegant and beautiful ladies when the door suddenly opened quietly and an old man came in, one hand stroking his silvery beard, the other carrying a gleaming copper bucket of shit... With a graceful gesture the venerable old man placed the bucket on a chair, at which the ladies bent forward, lorgnettes at the ready.

With a triumphant expression, the silverbeard removed the bucket lid. What happened next was like a speeded-up film: a herd of antelopes fleeing from a roaring lion could not have taken flight more quickly than my fair guests. I waited, wordless, for the terrible ancient to break the silence. 'For a long time I was afraid to come, but since it's such a lovely day . . . Look, squire, a lump the size of your head. And I didn't clean it up, so you can see it's genuine . . .'

Following the instructions, I heated the base matter for weeks at a constant low temperature and, to the great surprise of both myself and my chemical adviser, the inexplicably beautiful changes in colour took place right up to the peacock sheen. One day, while I was standing by the retort, it exploded and the 'matter' flew in my face. I repeated the experiment, but with an open retort . . . It is completely incomprehensible why that one should explode as well – and at precisely the moment when I was standing in front of it.

When I tried to repeat the experiment a third time I went down with a horrible disease, which is considered incurable and only slowly got better after many years. Since then I have refrained from practical alchemy; better superstitious than unhappy.

(*Latern*, 298–301)

How much truth can one accord such a story? Meyrink was certainly interested in alchemy, it forms an important theme in his final novel, *The Angel of the West Window*, and the author mentioned, Onuphrius Marsciano certainly existed; there is a similar but more matter-of-fact version of the story in his introduction to his translation of St Thomas Aquinas's book on the philosopher's stone. He also suffered from a serious illness, from which it took him years to recover, but the timing does not fit; elsewhere he says his serious illness broke out in 1897. The ironic tone of the narration makes the reader suspicious and it was written at a time when Meyrink was in serious financial difficulties, which accompanied him for much of his life: he was forced to sell The House by the Last Lamp in October 1928; 'How I Tried to Make Gold in Prague' was published in December of that year, 'Magic and Chance' in 1931.

Even if these stories are invented, there are others, recounted both by Meyrink himself and by apparently reliable and sober acquaintances, which have the ring of truth. One can well imagine that, given his notorious reputation in Prague, Meyrink might – might – write a spurious account of the alchemical or gambling exploits of his younger days, but there seems no reason to invent an episode such as the vision of a clock tower he recounts in 'Meine Erweckung zur Seherschaft' (The Awakening of my Clairvoyant Faculty).[3] It is to this more serious side of his interest in the occult that we will now turn.

The Pilot

Meyrink's transformation from dandy to serious seeker after esoteric truth took place gradually during the 1890s, but the

[3] *Merlin* 3/ 1949. The German text has not been collected, but there is a French translation by A.-D.Sampieri: 'Mon éveil à la voyance' in: Gustav Meyrink. ed. Yvonne Caroutch, Editions de l'Herne, Paris, 1976, pp. 113–118.

event that initiated it was dramatic. His account may have a touch of *self*-dramatisation, but the result was certainly genuine. There is another, very similar version of the event to the one below in 'The Awakening of my Clairvoyant Faculty', in which he says he was twenty-three at the time and suffering from a 'disappointment in love'. That, and the date he gives in 'The Transformation of the Blood' suggests the experience occurred in 1891, a year before his first marriage.

The Pilot

Tomorrow is the twenty-fourth anniversary of that day, the Feast of the Assumption. Sitting at my desk in my bachelor's room in Prague, I put the farewell letter I had written to my mother in an envelope and picked up the revolver on the desk in front of me. I intended to set off on my journey across the Styx, to cast away a life that seemed shallow and worthless, with no prospect ever of solace.

At that moment the 'Pilot with the mask of invisibility over his face', as I have since called him, boarded the ship of my life and swung the helm round. I heard a rustling at the door onto the landing and when I turned round I saw something white being pushed under the door across the threshold into the room. It was a printed pamphlet. That I put the revolver down, picked up the pamphlet and read the title was due neither to a stirring of curiosity, nor to some secret desire to postpone my death – my heart was empty.

I read: 'On Life after Death'.

'Strange coincidence!' The thought tried to stir in my mind, but the first word scarcely reached my lips. Since then I have not believed in coincidence, I believe in the Pilot.

With trembling hand – earlier it had not trembled for

one moment, neither when writing the farewell letter to my mother, nor when I picked up the revolver – I lit the lamp, for it had grown dark, and read the pamphlet – obviously pushed under the door by my bookseller's delivery boy – from beginning to end, my heart pounding. It was all about spiritualism, mainly describing the experiences those who had done important research in that area – William Cookes, Prof. Zöllner, Fechner and others – had had with various mediums: Slade, Eglinstone, Home etc.

I sat awake the whole night through until the first light appeared and burning thoughts, until then alien to me, were going round and round in my brain. Could such outstanding scientists as the aforementioned be mistaken? It was almost inconceivable. But in that case what strange, incomprehensible laws of nature, which made a mockery of all known norms of physics, had manifested themselves?

During that night the searing desire to see such things with my own eyes, grasp them with my own hands, to check their genuineness and comprehend the secrets that must lie behind them, burnt until it glowed with an inextinguishable white-hot flame.

I took the revolver, for the moment redundant, and locked it in the drawer; I still have it today. It has died of rust, the cylinder won't revolve any more, never will revolve again.

(*Latern*, 286–7)

The result of this was an outburst of frenetic activity:

I was obsessed with the idea of experiencing spiritualist phenomena. Any visionary, prophet or fool on the loose in Bohemia attracted me as an electrostatic rod attracts scraps of paper. I invited dozens of mediums and held seances lasting half the night at least three times a week with a few friends I had infected with my monomania.

(*Latern*, 289)

It was not only frenetic, it was sustained; Meyrink called these activities a 'labour of Sisyphus' lasting seven years.

There was plenty for Meyrink to investigate. The advances in science and technology plus what many saw as the increasing materialism of the 19th century had triggered off a counter-interest in spiritual matters. Much of this had its focus outside the established churches and there arose a plethora of small groups, religious conventicles (such as Meyrink portrays in *The White Dominican*), secret societies, mystic orders. The second half of the 19th century also saw the appearance of mediums who promised clairvoyant visions and messages from the 'other side'. Spiritualism became popular, indeed fashionable – Meyrink himself called it a 'spiritual epidemic'. (*Latern*, 230) Many country-house parties of the time played at table-rapping, ouija board seances or calling up spirits.

Meyrink tried them all. It was a remarkable search in which he displayed determination and stamina. Although he was keen to discover occult truths, he retained his critical faculties, quickly seeing through false mediums and religious cranks. An acquaintance says that when he attended a seance in the house of Baron Schrenck-Notzing, a wealthy and credulous amateur of psychical research, he snipped of a tiny piece of the ectoplasm the medium gave off to have it analysed. Later he warned, 'Today there are more clairvoyants that ever before; unfortunately their clairvoyance is mainly directed at how to get money out of their credulous and uncritical neighbours.' (*Latern*, 245)

Despite his disappointments, however, Meyrink also retained his belief that there was something beyond – or other than – everyday reality. And this belief was eventually rewarded. In 'Das Zauberdiagramm' (The Magic Diagram) he said:

> For years I held seances in Prague – probably several hundred – with the best mediums that were to be had. Always without success; everything I saw and experienced could be explained as conscious or unconscious delusion on the part of the subject. I was about to abandon my experiments when, by 'chance' . . . I witnessed such clear physical events produced by a medium in a haunted house in Levico that it was impossible for me to doubt any longer: there are, if only rarely, phenomena which completely overturn everything science claims to know about the laws of matter. Since then I have conducted no more experiments in spiritualism; what I have seen is sufficient for me.
>
> (*Latern*, 264)

He also seems to have continued his riotous living. The article on 'The Pilot' continues:

> My blood became hotter and hotter, all kinds of cravings ate away at me, a lust for life that I can hardly comprehend today reared up inside me, but when I woke up late in the morning after a night of wild dissipation (strangely enough, these usually followed directly on from spiritualist seances, as if psychic batteries of the worst kind had transferred their power to me), I was never affected by the bleakness of everyday life, was never struck with revulsion, disgust, or remorse: during the hours of sleep the mysterious bellows of the underworld of the soul had fanned the flames of longing for the world beyond the Styx into new life.
>
> (*Latern*, 290)

It is perhaps hardly surprising that the decade ended in serious illness.

He bought and read any books about spiritualism and similar topics he could get his hands on: 'Fate, in the form of booksellers, deluged me with specialist tomes.'[4] Eventually he built up an extensive library of the occult. His willingness to buy almost anything and everything must have made him a favourite customer of antiquarian booksellers who would doubtless welcome such instructions as those for the second volume of the treatise on alchemy in the catalogue of an auction in Milan: 'Buy whatever the price.' One suspects that his 'money's no object' attitude applied to other things as well and at least in part explains why his substantial inheritance had disappeared by 1902.

Just as he tried out every medium he could find, Meyrink joined many of the occult societies and mystic orders that sprang up, many in England, around the end of the century like mushrooms after autumn rain. He was admitted to a French order in 1892 and in 1893 was in correspondence with John Yarker, who had left the Freemasons and founded the English *Ancient and Primitive Rite of Masonry*, and with the Supreme Magus of the *Societa Rosicruciana in Anglia*, who told him, 'it is an absolute despotism, and one can only ask and never claim anything in the order.' In the same year he was received into the 'Mandale of the Lord of the Perfect Circle', the letter attesting 'that Brother Gustav Meyer of Prague be constituted one of the seven Arch censors' and giving him the 'Spiritual and Mystic name Kama'. In 1895 'Charubel', of Sefton St., Earl St., Manchester, informed him of his acceptance into a mystic brotherhood, which had its own alphabet. Meyrink was given the name 'Theaverel: this name, when translated in English, would be expressed thus: I go; I seek;

---

[4] Caroutch, p. 114.

I find.' A further letter included the formula for a mystic rite:
'It brings you dear Brother face to face with terrible reallities
[sic].' In 1897 he was accepted into the Order of the Illumin-
ati with the name of Dagobert. A letter from the *Bruderschaft
der alten Riten vom Heiligen Gral im Großen Orient von Patmos*
(Brotherhood of the Ancient Rites of the Holy Grail in the
Grand Orient of Patmos) is undated.

In 'What's the use of white dog shit', a piece first published
in 1908, Meyrink wrote:

> There can't be a single fraternity left that I haven't
> joined, and if I were to go through all the profoundly
> meaningful secret signs and emergency signals that I
> learned one after the other, I'd be carted off to the asy-
> lum for sure, suspected of having contracted St Vitus'
> dance.

> (*Opal*, 158)

Despite that, Meyrink resumed his interest in this kind of
society in the 1920s, as is attested by letters from a member
of the *Alt-Gnostische Kirche Eleusis* (Old Gnostic Church of
Eleusis) and (eight long letters) from a Meredith Starr of
Wadebridge, Cornwall, about his acceptance into the Aquarian
Foundation and the White Brotherhood. He was also still
(or once more) in contact with G. R. S. Mead of the Theosophical Society, which he left only three months after
having joined in 1891.

To the modern reader and, it seems clear, to Meyrink
himself, many of these correspondents were obvious cranks.
(I have to confess that my notes on these letters in the
Meyrinkiana archives in Munich frequently have the comment: 'Mad!') But as with the mediums, he was always pre-
pared to try in the hope that he might find what he was
looking for. In the event, he left the societies, orders and
brotherhoods almost as quickly as he joined them.

Whether the Theosophical Society consisted of cranks is a matter of opinion, but no one can deny its importance as a cultural phenomenon and its influence in the late 19th and early 20th centuries. Meyrink was one of the founder members of the Theosophical *Loge zum blauen Stern* (Lodge of the Blue Star) in Prague in 1891. He met the general secretary of the European section of the Society, G. R. S. Mead, in Vienna the next year. In a letter about a month later Mead tells 'My dear Meyer', 'I judged then [in Vienna where they first met] that you were a man not of words but of action.' It is perhaps an odd description, given Meyrink's voluminous correspondence and his reputation in Prague as a raconteur, but then Mead was asking him to help in setting up a lodge in Budapest. However, Meyrink's description of his activities during his time as a member of the Society fully justifies Mead's description:

I joined the Theosophical Society, founded a lodge in Prague and went round like a roaring lion to recruit members; I gave talks to a small group from English *siftings* and *pamphlets* [in English in the original]. The only lasting reward for all my efforts was that I eventually acquired an ability to translate extempore, so to speak, so that today I can read out aloud from an English book as if it were in German. Annie Besant rewarded me for my zeal by accepting me into a certain inner circle, the centre of which is in Adyar in India. I received a number of letters from her with instructions about yoga. From that moment until my resignation some three months later I led the life of man who was almost mad. I existed on nothing but vegetable matter, hardly slept at all, ate a tablespoon of gum arabic dissolved in soup twice a day (it had been most warmly recommended to me by a French occult order for the purpose of awakening astral clairvoyance) performed asana exercises (Asiatic sitting positions with crossed legs) for eight hours night after night, at the same time holding my breath until I was shaking fit to die. Then, at the new moon, I rode out in complete darkness to a hill known as the Cave of St Procopius outside Prague and stared at a point in the sky until it began to grow light.

(*Fledermäuse*, 212–3)

He quickly became disappointed with the Theosophical Society. Annie Besant's evasive replies to his questions about yoga convinced him her knowledge was superficial and some of the material he found in the Theosophical *siftings* he described as 'dreadful kitsch'. (*Fledermäuse*, 227) He talked of a 'Theosophical fashion' and in the archives is a plan for a 'Theosophical comedy' which would have made fun of the Society. In 'Fakirpfade' (The Paths of the Fakirs) he talks of the modern fashion for the occult in the course of which 'a cubic kilometre of mouldy manna in the form of Theosophical literature has fallen from the heavens.' (*Latern*, 232)

An interesting sidelight on his experiences with Theosophy is Meyrink's relationship with Rudolf Steiner. Meyrink met Steiner once and it is likely he heard (or at least heard of) the lectures he gave in Munich. Yet despite similarities in their outlook, for Meyrink Steiner seems to have been tarred with the Theosophical brush (he almost always uses the word 'Theosophy' for both that and for Anthroposophy). The minor character of Brother Ezekiel in *The Green Face* is based on Rudolf Steiner. A manuscript with Meyrink's notes says, 'Ezekiel becomes a medium, or a swindling exploiter ... Becomes famous as a prophet and bogus medium, or healer (Model: Steiner).' In his satirical grotesquerie *Meine Qualen und Wonnen im Jenseits* (My Torments and Delights in the World Beyond) he portrayed Steiner as Dr Schmuser (flatterer, lickspittle, toady):

66

I was still wandering through the meadows when the sight of a wondrous *fata Morgana* swept away the rest of my disgruntlement. It was the precise reflection of an earthly occurrence, only even more uplifting, if that were possible: Dr Schmuser, the incorrigible prophet-in-ordinary and founder of the theosophical-anthroposophical-rosicruci-pneumatotherapeutic society was taking his constitutional in the clouds, correcting with the one hand the galley proofs of the Akashic records the foreman of the cosmic works had entrusted to him, whilst tirelessly waving the other in greeting to the gods. Behind him was his guard of honour: twelve exquisitely affluent old ladies. Once more, I realised, he was leading the faithful; presumably he was escorting them to nirvana . . .'

(*Fledermäuse*, 148)

Steiner, it has to be said, displayed tolerance and a sense of humour. Instead of hitting back, as some of his supporters would have liked him to, he retained his positive attitude towards Meyrink as a man who had extraordinary access to the spiritual world.

The most striking example of Meyrink's determination to progress spiritually can be found in his relations with a Christian sect near Darmstadt calling itself Rosicrucian and led by a man with the mystical name of Brother Johannes. Johannes, it seems certain, was a weaver called Alois Mailänder. Meyrink says he could neither read nor write; certainly Johannes's many letters to him are written by other members of the sect, notably his wife. There are some forty letters from Johannes to 'Brother Ruben-Juda', the mystical name Meyrink was given. They are full of vague admonitions and advice that sound like the garbled regurgitation of clichés of mysticism (the semi-literate language does not help): 'The way is never fast, for the fruit within us must first be born ripe, only then can one make further use of its powers.' When Meyrink complained of a sore throat, Johannes interpreted it: 'As far as your *sore throat* is concerned, its spiritual meaning is: "You will harvest ripe fruits" (or: "Gain spirits from outside")' Much is even more banal, such as: 'Anyone can understand that it was very difficult for you; but all sufferings purify and have their good purpose, even if poor mortals in this world cannot see it.' (*Fledermäuse,* 408–10)

It is difficult to understand how Meyrink, who was so scathing about Theosophy, can have put up with this for thirteen years, but he claims he did so. His initiation into the order was in 1892 and the last extant letter from Johannes is dated September 1903; Mailänder died in 1905 and it was only at that point that Meyrink was released from his grip.

Johannes's 'method' was to get his disciples to repeat sentences to themselves, presumably together with physical exercises, or the adoption of some specific position:

> Day after day, without leaving a single one out, I practised the 'mantrams' for thirteen years with no result whatsoever ... In 1900, to celebrate the turn of the century so to speak, I was struck down with the most awful disease of the spine. Even today I still believe it was the result of 'J's' exercises.
>
> (*Fledermäuse,* 241)

Unlikely though it may seem, however, Meyrink's later assessment of his thirteen years of suffering had its positive side. Johannes – and other experiences during the decade 1890–1900 – changed the focus of Meyrink's search. He no longer looked outside himself for knowledge, for esoteric truth or for a spiritual being; increasingly he looked inside himself and saw himself as a whole: mental, spiritual and physical. As Smit points out, his experiments with drugs had shown him that, whatever experiences they provide, their end result is not the expansion but the splitting of the mind.[5] When practising breathing exercises, he instinctively fought against the self-hypnosis they were intended to induce for:

> if I had not done so I would today probably be an unhappy medium or would suffer from some kind of schizophrenia, perhaps even religious mania. As it was, I clung onto a valuable insight: always remain conscious!
> (*Fledermäuse*, 220)

And his final tribute to Johannes, admittedly written probably over twenty years later, emphasises that transformation does not mean overcoming the physical side of our being, but should include it:

> If I had learnt nothing more from this man than the knowledge that the body must be included in the transformation of a person through yoga, I would owe him my lifelong gratitude ... I can assure you that the teaching method of that 'guide' awoke an inner life, the richness and value of which no one who had not experienced something similar themself can imagine. This period of apprenticeship also included the change of the blood that compelled me to become a writer. Quite apart from other transformations which I cannot go into here.
> (*Fledermäuse*, 229–31)

Robert Karle, in his introduction to his edition of Meyrink's

---

[5] Frans Smit: *Gustav Meyrink: Auf der Suche nach dem Übersinnlichen*, tr. Konrad Dietzfelbinger, Munich, 1990, p. 43.

long essay on his spiritual development, 'The Transformation of the Blood', says that Meyrink used his experiences with Johannes in his portrayal of Klinkherbogk in *The Green Face*. (*Fledermäuse*, 440)

During the 1890s Meyrink tried many gurus, systems, sets of exercises, diets and drugs, but none led to the insight and release of spiritual energy he was looking for. However, as with Johannes, they do seem to have had an indirect effect on his spiritual development, they 'loosened up his inner self', as he puts it in 'The Transformation of the Blood' (*Fledermäuse*, 231). His first progress on the road was the awakening of his clairvoyant faculty:

One winter's night I was sitting on a bench by the Moldau. Behind me was an old bridge with a tower with a large clock. I had already been sitting there for several hours, wrapped up in my fur coat, but still shivering with cold, staring at the greyish-black sky, trying everything possible to attain what Mrs Besant had described to me in a letter as inner vision. In vain. From earliest childhood I had been surprisingly devoid of the faculty many people possess of being able to close their eyes and imagine a picture or a familiar face. It was, for example, quite impossible for me to say whether one or other of my acquaintances had blue, brown or grey eyes, dark hair or brown . . . in other words, I used to think in words, not in images. I had sat down on this bench with the firm resolution of not getting up again until I had succeeded in opening up my inner vision. My model was Gautama Buddha who had once sat under the Bo tree with a similar resolution. Of course, I only stuck it out for about five hours and not, like Him, for days and nights. Suddenly I wondered what time it was. Then, just at the moment when I was torn from my contemplation, I saw, with a sharpness and clarity with which

I could not remember ever having perceived any object before in my life, a huge clock shining in the sky. The hands showed twelve minutes to two. It made such a profound impression that I clearly felt my heart – not miss a beat, no, beat extraordinarily slowly. As if a hand were holding it tight. I turned round and looked at the tower clock, which until then had been behind me. It was impossible that I should have turned round earlier . . . for I had sat on the bench for five hours motionless, as is the strict requirement for this kind of concentration exercise. The clock, just like the one I had seen in the sky in my vision, showed twelve minutes to two. I was overjoyed; just a faint worry: would my 'inner eye' stay open? I started the exercise again. For a time the sky remained greyish-black and closed, as it had been before. It suddenly occurred to me to see if I could make my heart beat in as calm and controlled manner as it had done of its own accord when I had had the vision, or possibly, most probably even, *before* the vision. This did not occur to me the way things usually do, rather it was like a deduction or instruction from the sense of one of the Buddha's sayings which came to me as if from the invisible lips of the 'masked figure'. The saying was, 'things come from the heart, are born of the heart and subject to the heart.' Thanks to my yoga exercises I could influence my heart to a certain extent . . . Immediately I entered a state which had been completely foreign to me until then: an intense feeling of unusual wakefulness. At the same time I saw a circular piece of the night sky recede, as if a magic lantern were starting, as if it were coming away from the atmosphere and retreating into more and more immeasurable depths of space . . . In the round hole in the air was a geometrical sign. I did not see it as one normally sees things in the world, from the front or the side, I could see it from all sides *at once*. The sign was the so-called *in hoc signo vinces* = a cross within a capital 'H' . . .

(Fledermäuse, 213–6)[6]

With practice he found he could switch on this inner vision without even having to induce the state of calm, though he could not call up images at will. He saw this as proof that they came not from his conscious mind, but from deeper within himself. They were communications to him, warnings, advice, instruction, but *not* from some outside agency, from God or some being in the spirit world. The focus of Meyrink's spiritual search had changed from a search for outside knowledge to the release of spiritual forces that were already there, dormant within himself.

The 'Pilot' he mentions in the experience where he was saved from suicide sounds like a spirit guide such as mediums use. He also uses the term 'the masked figure' or 'the masked guide'. Whether he initially had something like a spirit guide in mind, is not clear, but Meyrink soon became convinced that it was not a personalised spirit. He also uses 'fate' as a synonym for the Pilot and also sees it as coming from deeper inside him, rather than as something imposed from outside. In the archives there is a document in the same bundle of papers as 'The Pilot' and written in the same handwriting entitled 'The Dream as Pilot', suggesting that he believed the invisible Pilot came from deep within his psyche, as does a dream.

Meyrink later claimed that this 'inner vision' turned into powers which he himself called magic. In the article 'The Magic Diagram' (*Latern*, 264–73) he recounts how a swami with whom he was in correspondence gave him a yantra, a diagram used in meditation, which could also be used to

---

[6] There is another version in 'Meine Erweckung zur Seherschaft', French translation in Caroutch.

recover lost objects. He had, the swami said, to visualise the object in the diagram and the object would return to him. Meyrink claimed it worked: on one occasion he happened to see a cigar-holder of his that had disappeared shown by one man to another in the street; on another an old pair of scissors of strange design that he had dropped into the Moldau were returned a few days later. In 'Magie im Tiefschlaf' (Magic in Deep Sleep) he tells how once, when he was travelling by train, he realised he had forgotten to tell his fiancée (later his second wife) something important: 'What I had to do now was to fall asleep as quickly as possible and imagine myself in Prague. Make my heart into a transmitter by slowing down my heartbeat.' (*Latern*, 280) At the same time his fiancée woke up in Prague and saw a vision of Meyrink raising his hand in warning. She then did everything Meyrink wanted. The caricaturist Thomas Theodor Heine described how, when he visited Meyrink at his little cottage on the Ammersee, he watched him cast fishing nets murmuring something that sounded like 'Yi linho buttan rah'. The catch was too large to get all the fish in the boat. 'Now can you understand why the fishermen are angry?' Meyrink said. 'They're afraid I'll fish the lake empty, they say I'm a sorcerer.' (*Fledermäuse*, 426)

A journalist, pen-name Kemil Oraj, described how Meyrink was annoyed that a huge oak tree in the neighbouring garden spoilt the view from his house in Starnberg. The neighbours refused to cut it down, despite being offered a considerable sum of money, so Meyrink decided to remove it by magic. He told a friend it would be gone by the next new moon. On the day before that there was a great storm and the oak was struck by lightning. Meyrink was pleased that something had happened, but disappointed that the tree appeared scarcely damaged. He continued with his magic and several weeks later Oraj had a phone call from him: the tree had disappeared overnight. It had been sawn off and all the wood vanished without trace. The neighbours, furious, made enquiries. Men going to work early had seen an unknown man leading a horse-drawn cart filled with wood; he was never found. Oraj does preface his article, which was published after Meyrink's death, with the remark that 'people who visited Meyrink could not tell when he was exaggerating, being ironic, joking and when he was speaking of things he meant seriously, things that were true, with a smile on his face. (*Fledermäuse*, 427–430) Whatever the truth or not behind Oraj's story – and there are more similar ones both in his article and recounted by other people – it is characteristic of the way Meyrink was seen by those around.

4

The End of Life in Prague

Illness

The end of the century brought the end of Meyrink's happy-go-lucky life in Prague. By 1904, when he was forced to leave, he had lost both his health and his wealth.

In 'The Transformation of the Blood' Meyrink said, 'In 1900, to celebrate the turn of the century so to speak, I was struck down with 'the most awful disease of the spine'. (*Latern*, 241) Meyrink is clearly making a kind of joke of the date. A document in the archives gives the date as 1897 and is more convincing in that the date itself is incidental. In the margin of the horoscope mentioned earlier, he wrote, 'Start of illness 1897 – spring 1899 outbreak. Life in danger 17th October 1905.' In 'How I Tried to Make Gold in Prague, published in 1928, but referring to events in 1893 or 4, he says, 'When I tried to repeat the experiment [making gold from faeces] for a third time, I was struck down by an awful disease which is considered incurable and which only abated after many years.' (*Latern*, 301) The similarity of phrasing in the two articles and the fact that they were written long after the event suggests that the more accurate date is probably the note on the horoscope.

Another possible explanation for the confusion over the date is that Meyrink also suffered from diabetes, which made him very weak: 'For a long time I couldn't write anything at all. I was so lethargic that for months I couldn't bring myself to leave the house.' (*Fledermäuse*, 268) The horoscope dates might refer to that.

Given his reputation, rumour abounded: it was syphilis; it was caused by too much sport, by too much car-driving. Meyrink, as we saw earlier, attributed it to the exercises prescribed by Johannes. The doctors diagnosed it as tuberculosis of the spine. For some considerable time Meyrink, the well-known athlete, had difficulty walking and had to use sticks. The disease eventually relented and Meyrink could once again row, sail and climb mountains, though he was left with a slight limp. Towards the end of his life it became more acute again.

Although the doctors gave up his spinal disorder as a hopeless case, he did recover from his illness sufficiently to lead an active life, 'but that result was of secondary importance to me, the *way* I got rid of it through yoga, *that* was the key thing for me.' (*Fledermäuse*, 247) His experience with diabetes was similar, at least so he claimed. Despite his deep distrust of the medical profession, his wife eventually persuaded him to do something about it:

> I had to swallow my pride and go to the doctor. For two years I followed his advice and lived on nothing but blotting paper, so to speak. True, the sugar stopped, but my weight dwindled too. You'll be able to levitate after all, I mocked myself. Just a few dozen kilograms less and it'll be easy.
>
> (*Fledermäuse*, 269)

Since the doctor's 'cure' only seemed to make his general condition worse, he resumed the breathing exercises and bodily postures of Hatha Yoga he had abandoned. The result was not simply that his illness was cured, he came to a more profound understanding of the yogic exercises and found that they had positive effects far beyond the mere treatment of illness:

I imagined I had found the key: standing motionless on one leg ... is a balance exercise. And why exercise balance? I didn't work out that final puzzle straight away. I solved it by performing the exercise. Naturally I wobbled this way and that. But then – initially it was scarcely noticeable – the sensation of a 'union' arose, of a union – it is difficult to describe, I have no other word for it – with myself! Soon I could produce this remarkable sensation without having to stand up. The memory alone reawakened it. And by awakening that strange feeling of union I finally managed to get my diabetes to start to disappear, so that today I can live almost the same life, with no special diet, as a healthy person.

(*Fledermäuse*, 270)

The insight that his yogic exercises brought was similar to the one he had gained from the development of his 'inner vision'. Spiritual progress and enlightenment is not a matter of achieving knowledge, a simple physical facility or contact with some outside force, but of releasing the spiritual energy that was already there within himself. He continued to practise yoga for the rest of his life.

The Duel Affair

Duelling remained widespread in the Austro-Hungarian Empire up to the First World War, long after it had disappeared in Britain – and also long after it had been made illegal in Austria. Its illegality did not apply to duels between army officers, for whom it remained a 'sacred obligation', and the laws were not enforced if an officer was involved. An officer who killed a civilian was invariably pardoned by the Emperor. Duels were taken seriously and could result in the death of one party. Mark Twain commented: 'This pastime is as common in Austria today as it is in France. But with this difference – that here in the Austrian states the duel is dangerous, while in France it is not. Here it is tragedy, in France it is comedy.'[1]

All sources agree that Meyrink was a renowned duellist. As there appears to be no report of an actual duel, this presumably refers to his skill with the sabre. In the events referred to as the 'duel affair' he issued a challenge – or challenges; Strelka says he issued a public insult to the whole of the Prague officer corps and challenged any officer who sided with his opponents – but it was not accepted.[2]

As with many aspects of Meyrink's life, there are conflicting accounts of this business. Documents in the *Meyrinkiana* archives in Munich suggest the following course of events.

The matter arose, Meyrink explained in a declaration of December 1901, 'because Doctor Bauer deeply insulted me behind my back, at a time when he *knew* I was dangerously ill and therefore thought I *could not defend* myself.' Bauer rejected Meyrink's challenge on the grounds that, being illegitimate, he was incapable of 'giving satisfaction'. Meyrink regarded that as a further insult and took the matter to the military tribunal dealing with matters of honour. The tribunal upheld Dr Bauer's interpretation and declared Meyrink 'incapable of giving satisfaction'. Meyrink produced a document from the police stating that 'nothing to his disadvantage was known to them' and accused the chairman of the tribunal, a Captain Budiner, of lying. At the same time he consulted the authors of the military code of honour, who declared the decision of the tribunal invalid (one of them later withdrew his statement). In the meantime Captain Budiner and another officer brought a case of libel against Meyrink, which they won.

---

[1] Mark Twain: *Europe and Elsewhere*, New York and London, 1923, p. 225.
[2] Strelka, p. 8.

Meyrink was sentenced to fourteen days in prison, which was commuted to a fine. Meyrink, however, refused to accept this and appealed, claiming there had been collusion between Budiner and a policeman called Olič. Ten days later, on 18 January 1902, he was arrested on suspicion of fraud. He was kept in prison, awaiting trial, until 3 March; the arguments with the military honour tribunal continued for another year, until March 1903. Lube (182) states that Dr Bauer always said he could not attend because of work commitments, so that no conclusion was ever reached.

There is another version of the initial cause of the challenge that led to all the complications. According to Eduard Frank[3] it all started when a Herr Ganghofer, who belonged to the same rowing club as Meyrink, did not greet his wife when they met in the street. Meyrink remonstrated and eventually issued a challenge. From that point on the versions are the same. In another place Frank claims that Meyrink's future brother-in-law 'was his bitterest enemy'.[4] He does not relate that directly to the duel affair, but others must have done so, since Meyrink's second wife felt it necessary to issue a denial, in a letter to van Buskirk, presumably in the 1950s: 'There is *no* truth in the stories of the insult to his first wife, an argument with my brother.'

The Ganghofer story tends to degenerate into vague assertions and the documents indicate that Dr Bauer was the person involved in the 'honour tribunal' case. Frank does name Meyrink's seconds, a Count Resseguier and a Herr Kolischer, though they could have been his seconds against Bauer. What this whole affair does indicate is how touchy

---

[3] In his afterword to *Fledermäuse*, p. 423; there is a further variant in: *Prager Pitaval* (Berlin, 1931, pp. 326–8) by the journalist Egon Erwin Kisch; a long extract is printed in *Fledermäuse*, pp. 442–4.

[4] In his introduction to *Das Haus zur letzten Latern*, p. 11.

Meyrink was about his personal standing, presumably because of his illegitimate birth. His submissions on the matter, as in other cases, are detailed and emphatic, full of underlinings, suggesting an obsessive side to his nature. A newspaper report of his arrest said, not without a touch of *schadenfreude*, 'It has long been no secret for many people that Meyer, who is so touchy in certain respects, so determined in defence of his honour, is anything but a gentleman.'[5] Given Meyrink's prickliness, it is quite possible that there was another affair involving Ganghofer, which became confused in some minds with the real *cause célèbre*.

The duel affair was the beginning of the end of Meyrink's period in Prague and it does bring out a number of aspects of his life there: his dubious standing because of his illegitimacy and his consequent extreme sensitivity about his personal honour; the contradiction between his desire to be accepted by the upper reaches of society and his contempt for and deliberate flouting of certain elements within it; his reputation as an athlete, especially as a swordsman. There is even, in a story related by Ursula von Mangoldt, a connection between Meyrink's duelling and his dabbling in magic. Mocked for being a bastard, he would react aggressively with a challenge. Once an army officer lodged an official complaint and Meyrink was arrested (one of Meyrink's complaints to the honour tribunal was that an officer had reported a possible duel to the police, leading to him being warned and threatened with deportation). Shortly before being taken to prison he had buried an egg underneath an elder bush, an ancient form of magic. As it rotted, the egg was supposed to satisfy the demons of the world below and alter the balance between him and the officer at the place where the duel was to take place. Three days later, while he was waiting in his cell for the

[5] *Bohemia*, 19.1.1902.

duel, the news came that the officer had been fatally wounded in another duel. Meyrink was released. When he dug up the egg, only the shell was left. The contents had not rotted, they had completely disappeared.[6]

Prison

Although there is no actual documentary evidence, it seems probable and is generally assumed that Meyrink's arrest was instigated by the two army officers involved in the dispute, in collusion with a police officer. It was either an act of revenge on the part of the officers or a way of rendering Meyrink *hors de combat* – or both. It was greeted in some parts of the press with the kind of response that would lead to an expensive libel action today; a newspaper article of 1927 on the case even suggests that the rumours about Meyrink's actions were deliberately leaked to the press, presumably from official sources (see the reference to 'statements from the authorities' in one of the articles quoted below). The report in *Bohemia* quoted above continued:

> That Gustav Meyer's financial situation was not exactly sound was at least known to those who had to resort to distraint against him and only managed to recover their money with great difficulty or not at all. It happened more than once that Meyer, in order to conceal the fact that he did not even have a few stocks and shares, banknotes or coins for his window display, simply had the window repaired ... He naturally needed large funds to finance his normal lifestyle and he was truly

[6] Ursula von Mangoldt: *Auf der Schwelle zwischen Gestern und Morgen*, Weilheim, 1963, p. 97.

excellent at acquiring these, if not always by means of pure, honest banking business. Gustav Meyer was a 'spiritualist' and that explains why he had many women among his depositors. A horde of his agents travelled round Bohemia persuading credulous people to entrust their money to banker Meyer. They were told he was the son of a sovereign, his business was the leading Christian bank in Prague and his sole aim was to help the poor through skilful speculations . . . In all this Meyer was very cautious in his choice of customers; he sought them among the kind of people of whom he knew that for the sake of their name they would rather lose all their money than take legal action against him, in order to avoid trouble with the police and the courts.[7]

All accounts name the key figure in the accusations that led to Meyrink's imprisonment on suspicion of fraud as a senior police officer called Olič. According to the writer and journalist, Egon Erwin Kisch, who, together with Paul Leppin, is one of the main sources for this, in his appeal against the decision in the libel case brought by the two officers, Meyrink suggested there had been some kind of collusion between one of the officers and Olič. In the libel trial there had been suggestions that some of Meyrink's bank dealings were rather dubious and Olič used this to instigate the investigation. Some sources also claim that Olič fancied the woman who later became Meyrink's second wife, Mena Bernt, who was appearing as a singer in the *café chantant* of a Prague hotel. It is interesting, though entirely irrelevant, that Guillaume Apollinaire, in a piece called 'Le passant de Prague' (The Passer-by in Prague) set in March 1902, says that 'the

---

[7] *Prager Tagblatt* 21/1/27.

ground floor of the hotel I had been told about was occupied by a *café chantant*.[8] Could he have observed Mena singing there?

Meyrink was kept in prison for the two and a half months the investigation lasted. Kisch claims that three hundred witnesses were heard. All sorts of accusations were made: people who had put their money in Meyrink's bank could not get it back; he used his customers' stocks and shares for his own speculations, and, of course, that he used his occult powers to influence customers. Another accusation, that he claimed to be the son of Ludwig II of Bavaria, led to a search of his apartment.

There are also stories of bribed witnesses. Leppin says a Hungarian was put forward to claim he had deposited a share certificate with Meyrink, but when he asked for it back, Meyrink claimed never to have had it. Another version is that it was a woman who had deposited a security with Meyrink, which had disappeared. When asked for the serial number, she could not remember it and when asked to describe the shape and colour of the document she realised the game was up and made herself scarce.

In the end Meyrink was cleared of all charges. Max Brod's father was one of those who examined the books of Meyrink's bank:

Enemies . . . had accused him of dishonesty in his business affairs and reported him to the state prosecutor's office. Quite unjustly, as my father told me. And he ought to have known, for he was an accountant, at that time already deputy manager of a large bank; and he was one of those who had been charged with examining the

8 Guillaume Apollinaire: 'Le passant de Prague' in: *L'Hérésiarque et Cie*, Paris, 1967, p. 11.

books of the firm of Meyer. All the reports agreed:
no impropriety had been found.[9]

There is a document in the *Meyrinkiana* confirming this:

It is hereby officially confirmed that the preliminary
investigation against Herr Gustav Meyer, former banker
in Prague, on suspicion of fraud, which was opened on
18 January 1902, was abandoned on 2 April 1902 following a declaration from the state prosecutor's office
that they found no reason to continue the investigation.

Meyrink was completely exonerated but ruined. During
the investigation, his bank had been closed. It never reopened;
after the scandal and sensational reports in the newspapers
people were not surprisingly no longer willing to entrust
their money to him. In typical fashion he refused to accept
that and made desperate attempts to re-establish his good
name by asking the newspapers, who had been so quick to
condemn him, to print a statement that his books had been
found to be in order. Only a few printed a brief version; the
response of some was scornful. One is said to have written:

Outrageous. Gustav Meyer – the notorious owner of a
bureau de change who, after a series of problems with
the courts in January of this year, was arrested on
account of various widely publicised financial dealings
and released because at present the law has no precise
provisions for such 'dealings' – has, after having been
fortunate enough to escape retribution by the skin of his
teeth, had the impu – . . . imprudence to threaten to
take the editors of the newspapers, which reported on

[9] Brod, p. 294.

his doings on the basis of statements from the authorities, to court – for libel. One would imagine that this
type of person, only just having avoided the sword of
Damocles, would be happy to sink back discreetly into
social obscurity.[10]

The investigation had ruined his business and the period in
prison had aggravated his ill-health. According to Kisch it
took one more misfortune to drive him out of Prague. The
court hearing Meyrink's appeal in the libel case brought
against him by the two officers upheld the decision of the
original court and even insisted he should serve the prison
sentence, rather than pay a fine. Meyrink gave up, though he
did not move immediately, as Kisch implies. It was the next
year, 1904, that he left Prague for Vienna.

The experience of prison made a deep mark on Meyrink.
Soon after his release, or perhaps even while he was in prison,
he wrote two short stories which express the wretchedness
and despair of incarceration. The September 1902 number of
Simplicissimus, after his release in April, carried a piece by him
called 'Das ganze Sein ist flammend Leid' (The Whole of
Existence is a Blaze of Suffering) – the title is taken from
a poetic translation of one of the sayings of the Buddha:
'Sorrowful are all composite things. He who perceives the
truth of this gets disgusted with this world of suffering. This
is the path to purity.'[11] Old Jürgen's feelings in his cell
presumably reflect Meyrink's closely:

The warder went from door to door with his heavy
bundle of keys, shone his torch one last time through the
barred openings, as is his duty, and checked that the iron

[10] *Politik*, 22.4.1902; quoted in *Prager Tagblatt*, 21.1.1927.
[11] Tr. Harischandra Karivatna, Theosophical Society Press Online.

bars had been put across the doors. Finally the sound of his steps died away and the silence of misery descended on all the unfortunates who, robbed of their freedom, slept on their wooden benches in the dreary cells.

. . .

During the first weeks the feeling of outrage, of furious hatred at being locked up for so long when he was completely innocent had pursued him even in his dreams and often he had felt like screaming out loud in desperation.[12]

The prisoner is released and makes a meagre living selling caged songbirds until one day a woman brings two nightingales back and asks him to put out their eyes so they will sing more often. The man releases all his caged birds and hangs himself.

Before that, less than three months after his release, 'Terror' appeared in *Simplicissimus*. In it a prisoner in the condemned cell sees the terror he feels at his approaching execution as

a hideous worm . . . a gigantic leech. Dark yellow in colour, with black flecks, it sucks its way along the floor, past each cell in turn. Alternately growing fat and then elongating, it gropes its way along, searching.'

(*Opal*, 42)

In his first novel, *The Golem*, the hero, Pernath, is also unjustly imprisoned due to the machinations of a police officer called Otschin, a name which has deliberate echoes of Olič.

---

[12] Gustav Meyrink: *Des deutschen Spießers Wunderhorn*, ed. with afterword Gerhard Böttcher, Berlin, 1969, pp. 156–7.

5

Meyer becomes Meyrink

Meyrink was christened Gustav Meyer. It was only when he started publishing his stories that he took the pseudonym of Meyrink, which was said to be an older version of the family name. The reason for using Meyrink as a pseudonym, he said, was that 'I shared it [Meyer] with rather too many people.'[1] Being called Meyer, or one of its variant spellings (Maier, Mayer, Mayr, Meier), in German is rather like being called Smith in English. (His grandfather's name is given as 'Mayer' on his marriage certificate.) In 1917 Meyrink, his wife and children were given permission to change their name to the one he had so far used as a pen name:

Royal State Ministry of the Interior.

To the Royal Government, Interior Section, Upper Bavaria.

Re: Change of surname.

'On this 8th day of July in the year of our Lord 1917, it has pleased His Majesty the King of His sovereign power to grant such persons as are named on the following page the right to adopt and henceforward bear the surnames there noted, without prejudice to the rights of third parties. The fee is set at 100 marks.

---

[1] Francis: 'Meyrink erzählt aus seinem Leben', *Hannoverscher Anzeiger*, 18.10.1931.

Meyrink's biographers generally associate his transformation from banker to writer with the catastrophic events of
1901–03. His misfortunes certainly meant that he needed
another source of income and his writing provided that. He
had clearly told Johannes this, for in a letter of December 1902
his 'guru' said, 'I am happy that as far as material things are
concerned you can eke out an existence by writing articles.'
Though poor and with his mind on higher things, 'Johannes'
was not naive in financial matters. 'After the death of my wife, I
myself,' he told Meyrink, 'invested what little money I had in a
life annuity, so that I have enough for the essentials and am not
dependent on others.' (*Fledermäuse, 409*) Whether Meyrink
himself had earlier supported Johannes is not clear, but many
of the other 'mystical orders' he joined insisted on financial
contributions, or gave heavy hints they would be welcome.

When discussing how he became a writer, Meyrink himself
concentrates on the inner change. He relates this to his
experience sitting on a bench by the Moldau, when his inner
vision was awakened:

> This ability to see was the first reason why I became a
> writer . . . Initially the ideas that moved me to write
> fantastic stories were always images, situations or figures
> I had seen in a vision. They were the core around which
> I wove the stories.[2]

In his autobiographical article 'The Transformation of the
Blood' he again relates this awakening of his inner vision to
his becoming a writer:

> The faculty of inner vision which I acquired or opened
> up during that winter's night was, by the way, the first

[2] 'Bilder im Luftraum', quoted in: Manfred Lube: 'Tiefseefische', *Österreich
in Geschichte und Literatur*, 1971, vol. 9, p. 276.

decisive point in my destiny that changed me, at a stroke
so to speak, from a businessman to a writer. Previously
I had thought in words, from then onwards I could also
think in images; in images which I saw as if they were
really there before me; no, a hundred times more real,
more immediate than any physical object.

(*Fledermäuse*, 217)

The awakening of this faculty came during the time when
he was still dealing with Annie Besant of the Theosophical
Society, that is, presumably in 1892–3, so the 'all at once' will
refer to the arousing of his *ability* to write fantastic stories, not
that he actually started then. Later on in the same essay he sees
his experience on the bench by the Moldau as the first step on
the journey which was completed by what he learnt from
the teachings of Brother Johannes: 'My apprenticeship [with
Johannes] also brought the transformation of the blood which
compelled me to become a writer.' (*Fledermäuse*, 231)

When he actually started writing is uncertain. For a long
time it was assumed his first published story (October 1901)
was also the first he had written, but Manfred Lube identified
a short piece called 'Tiefseefische' (Deep-sea Fish) as having
been written in 1897. His friend, the writer Paul Leppin, who
was ten years younger and part of Meyrink's entourage in
Prague, said that Meyrink had earlier indicated his intention
to write a book:

It was shortly before the troubles that overtook him that
he occasionally declared his intention to write a book.
However, he never got beyond the announcement,
about which we were sceptical, even though he asked
concrete questions, quizzed authors and discussed the
craft with writers.[3]

[3] Leppin: 'Bankier Meyer'.

Meyrink himself cast doubt on the suggestion that he had started writing some years before his first published story. In one of his last interviews, which actually appeared two days after his death, he said:

I became a writer practically overnight . . . My sudden transformation surprised not only my circle of friends but myself as well. Until my first short story, 'The Ardent Soldier', appeared, I had never shown the least literary ambition.[4]

However, that was over thirty years after the event and he may have been more interested in bringing out the contrast between banker and writer, rather than in establishing the precise truth.

Recalling Meyrink, friends and acquaintances frequently mention the fact that he was a fascinating and compelling raconteur. Whether this ability to tell stories that gripped his audience was an ability that began with the awakening of his 'inner vision' or whether he had possessed it earlier, is impossible to say. But it is certainly connected with his appeal as a writer. His stories often have an immediacy which may well come, at least in part, from his preference for dictating rather than writing by hand. Later on he was one of the first writers to use the Parlograph, an early dictating machine which appeared around 1910. (An interesting sidelight is that Kafka's fiancée, Felice Bauer, worked for a 'Parlograph' firm.[5]) He may have been attracted by the idea of being in the forefront of fashion – one remembers that he claimed to have been one of the first to own a motor car in Prague – but it certainly

[4] Francis: 'Über die Gabe des "inneren" Gesichts', *Neues Wiener Journal*, 6.12.1932; French version: Caroutch, p. 237.
[5] Kurt Wolff: *Autoren, Bücher, Abenteuer*, Berlin, 1967, p. 18 (footnote).

suited his style of composition, allowing him to tell his stories as if he were recounting them to friends, rather than committing them to an impersonal sheet of paper.

The initial impulse to his career as a published author was given by another writer – whom he perhaps 'quizzed about his craft'. It was in a clinic in Dresden, where he had gone for treatment for his diabetes, that Meyrink met Oskar A. H. Schmitz. Schmitz, five years Meyrink's junior, was a poet who had turned to prose in the later 1890s. At the time of their meeting he was working on a collection of short stories that would be published in 1902 under the title *Haschisch* and were illustrated by Alfred Kubin, who was Schmitz's brother-in-law, having married his sister Hedwig (who was a morphine addict).

In his essay 'Wie ich Schriftsteller wurde' (How I became a writer) Meyrink recalled:

> When I related a few remarkable things that had happened to me, he said, 'Why don't you write that?' – 'How do you go about it?' I asked. 'Just write the way you tell it,' he advised me. So I sat down and wrote the story 'The Ardent Soldier' and sent it off to *Simplicissimus*. It was accepted immediately.[6]

Schmitz described his encounter with the 'athletically slim gentleman' whose 'piercing blue gaze' struck him:

> Apart from that he looked rather conventional with his cropped blond moustache, dressed with an *English elegance* which was rare for us at that time. He had a slight limp and always used a stick.
> He was *a – by the way, Christian – banker from Prague*

[6] *Deutsche Zeitung Bohemia*, 10.12.1931.

and certainly the strangest person I had met up to that time. For example he claimed magic was possible, talked of secret initiations, lodges, adepts, displayed a comprehensive knowledge of Indian religions, practised yoga and was at the same time well informed on practical aspects of the modern world . . . The most surprising thing about my new acquaintance, however, was his *sharp wit* and the *unerring eye* with which he observed the world around.

Whenever he had regaled us with one of his remarkable, fantastic and humorous stories, I kept on encouraging him to write them down. At first he wouldn't hear of it, claiming he had not the least literary bent . . . In his first manuscript there were some primitive stylistic lapses, which I explained to him. Almost nothing needed changing in the second, the third I left untouched. We sent off all three to *Simplicissimus*. A reply soon came. The editors asked if there were more stories of that kind and proposed a contract as a regular contributor at a good salary. This provided the author with the opportunity he had long sought to give up banking.[7]

This is the only clear evidence that Meyrink had 'long sought' to give up banking. The meeting with Schmitz took place in the summer of 1901, at the time, that is, of his dispute with the officers, but before it led to serious legal consequences.

The story of the acceptance of Meyrink's first story by the magazine *Simplicissimus* is another the authenticity of which has been cast in doubt. Its source is Meyrink's friend, Alfred

---

[7] Oscar A. H. Schmitz: *Dämon Welt*, Munich, 1926, pp. 264–6.

Meyrink 'dressed with an English elegance'

Schmid Noerr, in whose version Schmitz's advice is rather more robust. His placing of the meeting in 1903 instead of 1901 does not necessarily invalidate his evidence:

Meyrink escaped the worries and troubles the Prague stock exchange was causing him with a trip to a spa in Dresden. There he met the writer, Oscar A. H. Schmitz. The conversation grew lively and Herr Meyer told Herr Schmitz stories from his colourful life in Prague until finally Herr Schmitz, whose fingers were on the pulse of literary life, could hold back no longer. 'Why don't you write that down. You've got pure gold dripping from your lips, just like Gold-Marie in the fairy tale.' Immediately Herr Schmitz gave Herr Meyer the address of *Simplicissimus* in Munich, though accompanied by the well-meaning advice not to present himself as plain Herr Meyer.

Not long afterwards there was an editorial meeting in Munich. The assistant editor, Geheb [actually Geheeb, MM], held a manuscript called 'The Ardent Soldier' sent in by a certain Gustav Meyrink from Prague. Geheb shook the paper he was clutching and sighed. 'This stuff was written by a madman. Pity, there's things about it that aren't bad. As it is: the wastepaper basket.'

Their lord and master, Ludwig Thoma, arrived late. Taciturn, wreathed in pipe smoke, he lounged in his chair and, bored with the deliberations of the editorial meeting, rummaged with the spike of his stick in the wastepaper basket. He skewered a manuscript, took it, read it and growled, 'What've we got here?'

Geheb replied dismissively, though with a shrug of regret, 'A madman's submission.'

Thoma: 'A madman? Perhaps. But a genius. Yes, yes, Geheb, genius and insanity. Remember the name

Meyrink. And write to ask him if he's got more of this kind of thing. We'll print it immediately.'[8]

Roda Roda, who later wrote plays together with Meyrink, confirms Ludwig Thoma's intervention, though in slightly less elaborate form. In his version three stories, by Meyrink, Roda Roda and Paul Busson,[9] were on the desk to be returned to the authors. Ludwig Thoma, bored, read them, thumped the table and said, 'You buggers've got no judgment at all.'[10]

Simplicissimus was a weekly that had been founded in 1896, on the model of French magazines such as *Gil Blas Illustré*. It was a satirical magazine, which concentrated on political and social matters, but also included literary pieces, poems and stories. Many well-known writers were among its contributors, such as Rilke and Hesse, and for a while around the turn of the century Thomas Mann was a subeditor. With its anti-establishment attitude and its large number of cartoons, it was the most outspoken and irreverent commentator on the affairs of imperial Germany. Its particular targets were the monarchy, the aristocracy, the army, the police, the church and nationalist politicians. Produced in Munich, it was strongly anti-Prussian. It was banned for a time in Austria and several numbers were confiscated in Germany – one in particular which had a cover illustration mocking Wilhelm II – which only served to increase sales. Editors and contributors spent periods in jail and Albert Langen, the publisher, lived in Paris for five years for fear of arrest.

Simplicissimus was the ideal home for Meyrink's pieces. Of the fifty-three stories he published between 1901 and 1908,

---

[8] *Wunderhorn* afterword, p. 186.

[9] Another writer who, according to the Manchester Guardian of 21.6.1929, suggested that 'Germany is becoming rather too morbidly preoccupied with intellectual insanity'.

[10] Roda Roda: *Roda Rodas Roman*, Vienna, 1950, p. 401.

thirty-seven first appeared there. They were an immediate success and collections in book form soon followed, *Der heiße Soldat und andere Geschichten* (The Ardent Soldier and Other Stories) in 1904, *Orchideen* (Orchids) in 1905 and *Wachsfigurenkabinett* (The Waxworks) in 1907. All these early stories were collected in the three volumes of *Des deutschen Spießers Wunderhorn* in 1913. The title is a satirical reference to the Romantic folk-song collection *Des Knaben Wunderhorn* (The Boy's Magic Horn); literally Meyrink's title means 'The German Bourgeois' Magic Horn', though it is most commonly translated as 'The German Philistine's Magic Horn'.

Meyrink quickly became one of the magazine's leading contributors. He was especially popular with the younger generation, including many of the writers and artists who would become part of the Expressionist movement. For Max Brod Meyrink's pieces were 'fantastic stories . . . which had electrified me when they first appeared in the magazine',[11] and Erich Mühsam describes how he and his friends would always rush out 'to buy the latest edition of the Munich review; if it contained a new piece by Meyrink, then we had material for several evenings of discussion.'[12] Conservative quarters criticised *Simplicissimus* as a bad influence on young people, one right-wing newspaper, the *Augsburger Postzeitung*, calling it 'a danger to school discipline.'

Meyrink's stories of this first period (1901–08) have various elements – the supernatural, the grotesque, the macabre, the occult, absurd animal fables, parody, irony, caricature – but common to almost all is their fantastic, non-realistic nature. In 'The Transformation of the Blood' Meyrink expresses his contempt for realistic art:

[11] Brod, p. 150–1.
[12] Erich Mühsam: *Namen und Menschen. Unpolitische Erinnerungen*, Leipzig, 1949, p. 127.

A writer is praised if he has a keen talent for the observation of nature and can put it on paper by means of ink. He's a wretched photographer, nothing more ... I know many painters and have made great efforts to explain to them that they wouldn't need a model if they only knew how to open their inner eye. They listened, uncomprehending. They prefer to make tracings of nature.'

(*Fledermäuse*, 218)

Many of these stories have a satirical thrust. The origins of much of Meyrink's satire clearly lie in his personal experiences in Prague. Sometimes there is an almost direct reference, as in the Captain Bortdiner, the inventor of an 'Automatic Honour Calibrator' in 'Wetherglobin', whose name and function clearly recall the Captain Budiner who was the chairman of the military court of honour; Meyrink's rancour could be long-lived: a lackey in his final, unfinished novel, *Das Haus des Alchimisten* (The Alchemist's House) is called Bortdiner. In 'Dr Lederer' there is a senior police officer:

who not only welcomed gifts of silverware at Christmas, but had furthered his career by industriously treating any *persona non grata* as a suspect ... The state prosecutor naturally pursued the matter on the recommendation of this police officer, even though the couple had not been caught *in flagrante*.

(*Wunderhorn*, 141)

The model for this is Olič, the police officer whose machinations, Meyrink believed, had been behind his arrest. Generally, however, the targets are representatives of what he felt was a bourgeois society with its smug philistinism. The doctors who failed to heal him are one favourite target, along with scientists who ignore reality if it doesn't fit in with their theories, and the clergy receive the occasional swipe as well. However, it is that most sacred of sacred cows in imperial Germany and Austria that comes in for his most devastating satire: the military.

Meyrink later claimed that the amusing, exciting, mystifying or satirical elements of his stories were merely a façade behind which he smuggled in his main concern, his interest in the occult:

> I admit my stories in 'The Magic Horn' might lead the reader to the mistaken assumption that I am merely playing with metaphysical problems . . . Adopting a mask was a subterfuge of mine; I wanted to worm my way into *Simplicissimus* in order to use it as a platform from which I could present a sacred cause to the public by the back door, so to speak.'[13]

This sounds suspiciously like the wisdom of hindsight. Although stories such as 'Der Buddha ist meine Zuflucht' (The Buddha is my Refuge) or 'Die Weisheit des Brahmanen' (The Wisdom of the Brahmin) might be seen as genuine treatments of the occult, in others such as 'The Truth-drop' or 'Die schwarze Kugel' (The Black Sphere) the satirical denouement seems to cancel out any serious occult element. In his late interview with Francis, Meyrink admitted his satires had a different source from his other writings:

> I have to admit that my predominantly satirical works have nothing to do with the gift of 'inner vision'; rather their inspiration comes from my profound revulsion for anything to do with militarism, the *pickelhaube*, leaden

[13] Reported by K. G. Bittner in an unpublished commemorative article quoted in Frank, p. 14.

thought devoid of heart, servility towards social conven-
tion and the world of the German petit bourgeois.[14]

Given the 'profound revulsion' that is behind Meyrink's
satires and his personal experiences at the end of his time in
Prague, it is perhaps not surprising that revenge is a motif in
several stories. Typical examples of perverted and sophisti-
cated revenge are 'The Man on the Bottle', 'St Gingolph's
Urn' and 'Der Albino' (The Albino). The story 'G. M.', in
which the hero takes revenge on the whole of Prague, has
already been mentioned above. This 'global vengeance' seems
characteristic of Meyrink and perhaps adds weight to the
story that he challenged the whole of the Prague officers'
corps. An interesting example of the 'global vengeance' story,
which also has prophetic overtones, is 'Petroleum, Petroleum'.

Dr Kunibald Jessegrim is an engineer who believes he has
been cheated out of his inventions by 'the baseless hatred of
the crowd, driven by slogans to oppose everything that did
not conform to dull mediocrity' and comes to see himself as
the Scourge of God with a mission to destroy the world. He
makes a fortune out of a new drug, mescalin, and buys land in
Mexico beneath which are huge reservoirs of oil. By blowing
up the rock walls which contain the oil, he causes it to come
to the surface and gradually cover the seas, so that the world is
faced with a future without rainfall, since there will be no
longer any evaporation to replenish the clouds. The final
image of army officers in gaudy uniforms being sent to mop
up the beaches with blotting paper is a grotesque adumbra-
tion of numerous contemporary oil disasters from Alaska to
the Orkney Islands. (*Opal*, 45–51)

Doctors, scientists, the clergy, the bourgeoisie are all objects
of Meyrink's satire in the stories that were eventually gathered

---

[14] Francis, 6.12.32; Caroutch p. 237.

in 'The German Bourgeois' Magic Horn', but the main and most frequent target was the military. He lampooned the army for its arrogance and stupidity. In a number of stories where it is not the main topic, there are casual sideswipes at the military 'mind'. In 'Das – allerdings' (Now that, on the Other Hand) a group of researchers into spiritualist phenomena have discovered that they are able to photograph the future. The scientific expert they have invited to examine their discovery is unconvinced. In spite of all their evidence, he finds a 'rational' explanation for each photograph until he is shown one of a man without a head. When it is explained that 'the man [in the photograph] went on to take up a *military career*' the professor is immediately convinced. He is so astonished at this proof of clairvoyant photography that all he can do is stammer, 'Now that, on the other hand . . .' (*Wunderhorn*, 208)

This story demonstrates one of Meyrink's satirical techniques. A story in one specific genre or on one specific topic – here the paranormal – is suddenly hijacked at the end to make a satirical point. Other examples with a similar twist at the end are 'Das verdunstete Gehirn' (The Evaporated Brain), which again portrays the military as brainless, and 'Coagulum' in which a 'buried treasure' turns out to be a fossilised officer's word of honour which is described by the bank as not being of any value at all 'even were it not fossilised or coagulated'. (*Opal*, 184)

These satires target the military, but more particularly army *officers*. In 'Die Erstürmung von Serajewo' (The Capture of Sarajevo) the king of the country fighting against the Austrians orders his men on pain of death *not* to shoot Austrian officers, the subtext being that without officers the men would make much more formidable opponents. But there is one story, and a number of comments by Meyrink, which attack not just the military but militar*ism*, the kind of militarism associated with Prussia and symbolised by the spiked helmet, the *pickelhaube*. Meyrink shared the anti-Prussian sentiments of the south Germans:

> My father, a minister of the King of Württemberg, played an important role in the 1866 [Austro-Prussian] war. His political ideal was a world without Prussians. I have inherited from him this revulsion towards everything that comes from north Germany . . . For me the Prussian is a man whose greatest pride is to have a swagger stick instead of a heart. Apart from that he may have all sorts of excellent qualities. But they are irremediably spoilt. By what? By the Prussian tendency to march four abreast and to regard the regimental sergeant major as creation's crowning glory.[15]

The title of the story 'Wetherglobin' refers to a serum made from castrated rams which, its inventor claims, 'when injected into youths with a low patriotism quotient . . . produced a kind of primary patriotic frenzy within a very short time.' (*Opal*, 218) During a research expedition to Borneo a number of orang-utans who have been injected with the serum escape from their cages. They immediately choose the stupidest as their leader, who sticks some gold paper to his backside and marches them in military formation through the jungle. When the inventor tries to market his product, one country (the German Empire is obviously meant) replies that:

> thanks to the traditional loyalty to the royal family, to quotations and patriotic songs memorised at an early age, as well as to cleverly designed and brightly coloured children's toys etc., the vast majority of the population was already in a satisfactory condition.

> (*Opal*, 221)

[15] Francis, 6.12.32; Caroutch 236–7.

Baron Varnbüler von und zu Hemmingen, Meyrink's father

Meyrink's aversion to things North-German included the writer Gustav Frenssen, whose novels he parodied mercilessly. Frenssen, from Dithmarschen, a rural district on the west coast of Schleswig-Holstein, was a practitioner of *Heimatdichtung*, sentimental and nationalistic novels set among the rural population and celebrating traditional values in opposition to modern urban life. He was later popular with the Nazis. Meyrink ridiculed his style as much as his attachment to 'blood and soil',[16] though he did not spare the southern variant of regional art either.

There are stories from this period which do not have a satirical edge. Some are grotesque or simply bizarre, such as 'What's the use of White Dog Shit', but the most striking group belong to the genre of the macabre. These tales generally focus on some gruesome anatomical object, such as the eyeballs transformed into jewels in 'The Opal' or the preserved brain in 'The Preparation'; 'The Waxworks' has an exhibition of monstrosities, some of which have been created by the sadistic surgical skills of Mohamed Daraschekoh, a figure who appears in several stories. The masterpiece of this genre is undoubtedly 'Dr Cinderella's Plants'. Driven by some unconscious compulsion, the hero investigates a mysterious house on the Malá Strana (Lesser Bank) in Prague. The climax is his sense of horror as he gradually realises that what he had thought was a trellis covered with creeping plants is, in fact, a network of human veins throbbing with blood:

> In amongst them countless eyeballs glistened horribly, sprouting alternately with hideous warty nodules like blackberries, and following me slowly with their gaze as

---

[16] *Jörn Uhl und Hilligenlei. Gustav Meyrink contra Gustav Frenssen. Zwei Parodien* (Jörn Uhl and Hilligenlei. Gustav Meyrink against Gustav Frenssen. Two Parodies), Munich, 1907.

I passed . . . all seemed to be parts of living bodies, fitted together with indescribable art, robbed of any human soul, and reduced merely to vegetative organisms.

(*Opal*, 109)

This is presumably the feature Franz Blei had in mind when he drew his satirical portrait of Meyrink for his *Great Bestiary of Modern Literature:*

The Meyrink is the only mooncalf which dropped to earth and which is now in captivity. It is occasionally put on show by its captor. For a while pregnant women were banned from viewing it, because of the occurrence of a few premature births caused by the shock.[17]

The macabre based on disjoint anatomical parts, especially internal organs, is so striking in these early stories that it seems to hold a personal fascination for Meyrink, especially if it derives from products of his 'inner vision', beyond its function as an element of fiction. It disappears from his later novels and stories as does, to a certain extent, the grotesque, though that is still occasionally used to introduce or emphasise the occult.

[17] *Austrian Fantasy* p.71.

6

Unsettled years

Vienna 1904–5

'Prague had been ruined for Meyrink. For that reason he left the city and went to Vienna in 1904.'[1] This is the general view, echoed by Qasim:

> After the collapse of his bank following his imprison-
> ment, Meyrink had no further interest in staying in
> Prague, not least because his attempt to restore his dam-
> aged reputation had virtually no chance of success. For
> the good citizens of Prague he remained an object of
> whispers and rumour.
>
> (Qasim, 59)

Although he made extensive use of Prague in his writings, right up to his final novel, *The Angel of the West Window*, his attitude to the city itself remained ambivalent. In a newspaper interview of 1922 he said, 'If someone were to ask me, "Would you like to be in Prague again?", I would reply, "Yes, but only in memory, not for one moment in reality." '[2]

Yet he did not leave Prague immediately after his release from prison and the collapse of his bank in 1902. Precisely when he moved to Vienna is not clear, but he was presumably

---

[1] Frank, *Latern*, p. 14.
[2] Interview in *Prager Tagblatt*, 2.6.1922.

there by May 1904, when he became editor of the recently founded magazine *Der liebe Augustin*. Whether he left Prague in response to an invitation to take this post, or whether he was already in Vienna and available, is not known. The latter possibility is implied by Josef Strelka, who goes on to say:

'Within a year [of his release from prison as a financially ruined cripple] Meyrink, suddenly restored to good health, was strolling down Vienna's Kärntnerstrasse, swimming in the Danube, winning races at regattas and setting off on a merry life as sales rep for a champagne factory.[3]

Strelka adduces no documentary evidence to support this, though the Austrian writer Anton Kuh, in an article published in the year of Meyrink's death, claimed he had worked for a time for a champagne company in Vienna. What is certain, is that Meyrink was the editor of the Viennese magazine from May 1904 until it ceased publication for financial reasons in November of that year.

The magazine, which appeared thrice monthly, was named after a legendary Viennese figure, a 17th-century jokester who ignored the plague raging at the time in Vienna and got so drunk he did not notice when he was tipped into a pit with the bodies of the plague victims. The next morning he woke up and continued on his merry way, undaunted and unscathed. From the notice in the first number it appears to have been originally intended as a satirical magazine: 'Armed with humour and satire, *Der liebe Augustin* will use word and image to combat all excesses in public life.'[4] When he took over as editor with the fifth number, Meyrink both changed

---

[3] Strelka, p. 9.
[4] Quoted in Lube, p. 16.

the main focus of the publication and improved the standard of its literary and artistic contributions:

> *Der liebe Augustin* is independent of all political parties and under its present editor, Herr Gustav Meyrink, will endeavour to publish the best in literature and illustration.
>
> Free unbound imagination, humour and satire; a forum for genuine ability. Nothing forced, nothing crude or trivial; the greatest artistic freedom for all contributors.[5]

He published contributions from his Prague circle of friends, for example Paul Leppin and Max Brod, but he also commissioned work from some of the leading figures in contemporary German writing such as Otto Julius Bierbaum, Frank Wedekind, Paul Scheerbart, Peter Altenberg. There is even a story that he went to the Café des Westens in Berlin (where Rupert Brooke wrote 'The Old Vicarage, Grantchester') to solicit contributions.[6] He also included translations of authors such as Strindberg, Verhaeren (translated by Stefan Zweig), Jens Peter Jacobsen, Maeterlinck, Dante Gabriel Rosetti and Poe.

The range and quality of the illustrators he engaged were similarly impressive. Acquaintances from Prague included Hugo Steiner-Prag and Richard Teschner, who figured in *The Golem* as the puppeteer Zwakh. Others who contributed were Alfred Kubin, John Jack Vriesländer, who appeared in *The Golem* under his own name, the Berlin artist Heinrich Zille and representatives of the art nouveau *Secession* in Vienna, Josef Hoffmann and Kolo Moser.

---

[5] From the 17th number, quoted in Lube, p. 18.
[6] Mühsam, p. 100.

Not surprisingly, the increase in quality entailed a corres-
ponding increase in expenditure which eventually went
beyond what the proprietor was able, or willing, to afford. The
magazine folded after the eighteenth issue. Meyrink's bold
declaration of intent quoted above appeared in the seventeenth issue and was more a plea for help, especially the final
sentence, which ran: 'Does not such a magazine deserve to be
welcomed by the public?'

What Meyrink's somewhat extravagant editorial policy
does indicate is that, in Vienna as in Prague, he was very much
involved in the cultural scene. After the collapse of his bank in
Prague, he received financial support from Fritz Wärndorfer.
Wärndorfer came from a wealthy family of industrialists and
was one of the most important patrons of art at the turn of
the century; in particular he was involved in the *art nouveau*
movement. He commissioned a music room from Charles
Rennie Macintosh and was the one who financed the setting
up of the *Wiener Werkstätte*, the craft workshop and retail out-
let of the *Secession*. It was presumably through Wärndorfer
that Meyrink came into contact with Josef Hoffmann and
Kolo Moser.

But Meyrink was clearly able to keep out of the rivalries
that characterised the art scene in Vienna at the time, since he
was also on friendly terms with the architect and harshest
critic of *art nouveau*, Adolf Loos. Loos claimed he came across
Oskar Kokoschka when the latter was 'working for the *Wiener
Werkstätte* and was employed in the German manner – art in
the service of commerce – painting fans and drawing picture
postcards'.[7] Construing this as 'one of the greatest crimes
against the Holy Spirit' he set about trying to find commissions for Kokoschka. One of these was a portrait of Meyrink.

---

[7] Adolf Loos: *Ornament and Crime*, ed. Adolf Opel, tr. Michael Mitchell,
Riverside, 1998, p. 191.

It was done around 1910 and did not please Meyrink who, Ursula von Mangoldt, a younger neighbour in Starnberg, claims, hung it in the lavatory.

Another friend of Meyrink's in Vienna was Friedrich (Fritz) Eckstein. Like many of Meyrink's friends (as well as his enemies) he ran the risk, if risk it was, of appearing in his stories. In 'The Truth-Drop' the hero, Hlavata Ohrringle goes to consult 'an old adherent of the Rosicrucian Order, a certain Eckstein'. (*Opal*, 99) Eckstein was an important figure in Meyrink's development and a remarkable person in his own right. He founded the first official lodge of the Theosophical Society in Austria in 1887 and was acquainted with Meyrink from the time he helped to set up and briefly belonged to the Lodge of the Blue Star in Prague. He was a wealthy industrialist who had a wide range of interests – he was a private pupil of the composer Anton Bruckner and for a time his private secretary. In Vienna he had the reputation of knowing everything. There was, it was said, no question he could not answer immediately, though that may have come as much from his quick-wittedness as his fund of knowledge. Once, according to Friedrich Torberg, when out for a walk with Hugo von Hofmannsthal, a bird kept hopping along in front of them. Eckstein immediately identified it as an 'Egyptian king hopper', a kind of hoopoe which, he said could not fly, only hop, and spent the winter in Egypt. When Hofmannsthal reminded him that he had said it could not fly, he calmly replied, 'Oh, it can fly *that* far.'[8]

He had extensive knowledge of various religious and esoteric traditions (probably more than of ornithology); he was the friend Sigmund Freud referred to in *Civilization and its Discontents* as the one who had instructed him in yoga. Meyrink, too, profited from his knowledge of the occult and

[8] Friedrich Torberg: *Die Tante Jolesch*, Munich, 1977, p. 151.

mysticism. Eckstein was also the centre of a literary circle (including Trotsky) that gathered in a Viennese coffee house and it was there that Meyrink met writers such as Peter Altenberg and Paul Busson. His time in Vienna was relatively short, however. By the end of 1905 he had left Austria. His departure, according to Smit (80) was more of a flight – from a prison sentence of three years to which he had been condemned for his attacks on the military in *Der liebe Augustin*.

There followed an unsettled period for Meyrink, as far as his residence was concerned, but at least his personal affairs were settled. His first wife was finally persuaded by a mutual friend to agree to a divorce, which went through on 1 February 1905, allowing Meyrink to marry Mena Bernt, to whom he had been engaged since 1897. The marriage took place in Dover, presumably to avoid gossip, on 8 May 1905.

Montreux 1905–6

When he left Vienna, Meyrink went to Montreux. As usual, the precise date is unknown. There is an unfinished short story called 'Ismael Hannekamp' in the archives, which is set near Montreux and contains a letter dated 'Les Avants [near Montreux], 7 November 1905'. A sentence that was later crossed out suggests the narrator heard the story 'in the smoking room of a hotel in Montreux'. As Manfred Lube points out (19), with Meyrink's propensity for using personal experiences in his stories, this is a good indication that he was in Montreux by November 1905. The Meyrinks' daughter Sibylle was born in Montreux on 16 July 1906. That is the last documentary evidence for his stay in Montreux. By January 1907 he was in Munich.

Why Meyrink chose Montreux is also unknown. A possible link is his friendship with the architect, Adolf Loos, who

Meyrink with his second wife

was building a house near Montreux between 1903 and 1906. Meyrink's ironic description of the overelaborate architecture of the town is strikingly close to the attitude of Loos, whose equation of ornament with crime is one of the key statements of early twentieth-century architecture. In 'Montreux' Meyrink wrote, not holding back on the irony:

> The sight of the hilly landscape, with its covering of vines, that separates the town from the mountains is as refreshing and charming as that of a well-trimmed poodle . . . And how magnificently these bosky vineyards suit Montreux with all the sophisticated, refined luxury of its villas, hotels and guest houses!
>
> Adorned with a thousand little turrets they stand, these artistic buildings, with their proliferation of rampant arabesques. There is not one spot that the fertile imagination of the plasterer has forgotten to cover lovingly with ornamentation.
>
> (*Wunderhorn*, 197)

The *lack* of ornamentation distinguishing Loos's house near Montreux brought the wrath of the authorities down on him:

> I was all unsuspecting when, like a bolt from the blue, I received a summons from the planning authorities, who asked me what I, a foreigner, thought I was doing desecrating the beauty of Lake Geneva. The house was much too plain. Where was the ornamentation? My mild objection that on calm days the lake itself was smooth and unornamented and people still found it quite nice was brushed aside. I was given a certificate stating that it was forbidden to build such a house for the reason of its simplicity and therefore ugliness. Overjoyed, I made my way home.
>
> Yes, overjoyed! Is there any other architect in the

whole universe who has it in black and white from the authorities that he is an artist?[9]

Why he spent at least a year in Montreux is a mystery, perhaps even to Meyrink himself, as he makes a joke about it in his article 'Montreux': 'If someone were to interrupt me at this point and ask, 'Why did you stay there so long, then?' I would have to answer, 'Because I wanted to wait for the rain to stop.' (*Wunderhorn*, 195) His attitude to Switzerland is not very complimentary, either. An unfinished and uncompleted satire begins:

> Once upon a time there was a poor shepherd boy who, presumably as punishment for some grievous sin he must have committed in a previous existence, lived for a period of time in Switzerland.[10]

After a long and arduous journey under the ground, the poor shepherd boy comes face to face with one of the highest dignitaries of Switzerland in person, Guillaume Rülpsli – Guillaume is William, of course, and *rülpsen* is to burp in German.

His description of Montreux ends with a bizarre image of the Englishwoman abroad:

> Anyone looking up at the mountain ridge will see the Hotel Caux many hundreds of metres above Montreux. It looks down on the valley, encircled by a gigantic wall and built in the speculator style, half gingerbread castle, half sanatorium.

[9] Adolf Loos: *On Architecture*, sel. & intro. Adolf and Daniel Opel, tr. Michael Mitchell, Riverside, 2002, p. 70.

[10] 'Schweizer Mysterien', manuscript dated Starnberg 9.7.26 in the *Monacensia* archives in Munich City Library.

Like a lunatic asylum from the Arabian Nights!

Around Christmas the London shopkeeper's wife and daughters go tobogganing up there.

Like furies they hurtle down the slopes, baring all their sixty-four teeth. Sitting astride little wooden things that at first sight look like bidets on runners, but are only common-or-garden sledges.

Once they've managed to kill themselves, they get themselves soldered in, sent to London and buried at home.

(Wunderhorn, 201–2)

His reasons for leaving Montreux are no clearer than his reasons for going there in the first place. Buskirk mentions unpaid bills which had been reported in a local newspaper. This suggestion is supported by a letter in the archives of Munich City Library. It is from a lawyer representing an inhabitant of Montreux, who had taken Meyrink to court, presumably for non-payment of a debt; Meyrink's earnings from his contributions to the periodical *März* had been frozen, pending the court's decision. It went against him and the letter informs Meyrink and the publisher of the amount to be deducted from his royalties.

Munich 1906–11

When Meyrink left Prague, the obvious place for him to go would have been Munich. He presumably went to Vienna because of connections which provided work for him there; why he went to Montreux is unknown, if it was not connected with his friendship with Adolf Loos. Not only had he spent the first twelve years of his life in Munich, that was where he officially 'belonged'. He was registered in Vienna as a subject of the German Empire, specifically of the Kingdom of Bavaria. Presumably his mother had taken him back to Bavaria, after his birth in Vienna, and registered him there (one official document 'confirms that he is Bavarian, and that through descent'). It was the Bavarian army that rejected him as 'mentally unsuitable'. A *Heimatschein* – a certificate of right of residence – for the city of Munich was issued to him in April 1906, when he was in Montreux and had not even resided in Munich for over twenty-five years. Lube (20) suggests this might have been connected with the intention of settling in Munich; this is quite possible, as the certificate states that it is 'not valid for a stay outside the kingdom [of Bavaria]'. At that time, however, a *Heimatschein* from one's original place of residence was needed if one wanted to settle elsewhere and it is quite possible Meyrink applied for the Munich certificate to fulfil a requirement of the Swiss authorities, despite the restriction on the certificate when it arrived.

Perhaps more important than this official status was the fact that *Simplicissimus*, with which he had a contract as a regular contributor, had its offices in Munich. One might imagine he would value closer contact with his publisher and editors. However, Meyrink was very much his own man when it came to deciding what to write and how to write it, and it is quite likely that he preferred to keep at a distance from the day-to-day running of the magazine. Individual numbers of *Simplicissimus* often had a set theme and contributors were asked for pieces on the subject. Meyrink's story 'The Automobile' (*Opal*, 128–134) was written for the motoring number, and a number on the famous case of the 'captain' from Köpenick, near Berlin, in which simply by putting on a captain's uniform a man got people to obey him automatically and escaped with 4,000 marks, was just made for Meyrink. His contribution was 'The Evaporated Brain'. In it an officer (perhaps a bogus one, his name means something like 'Baron Swindler', but that may just reflect Meyrink's opinion of real officers) visits a scientist who is experimenting with brains

118

and drops his helmet on one of the objects of the scientist's research. When the scientist removes it, the brain has been transformed into a mouth, just a mouth, and a moustache with the points going up at right angles, like the Emperor's. A military helmet has the effect of making the brain evaporate. (*Wunderhorn*, 169–78) At other times, when there was to be a Rembrandt number, for example, he felt unable to contribute. The impulse behind his short stories is often very personal and he probably felt too constrained by having a subject dictated to him. He did at least manage to turn his motoring piece into a savage satire on the smug arrogance of the scientist. Although he had a permanent salaried position with the magazine, he did at times have to apologise for the lateness or lack of his contributions. He may have felt it was better not to be *too* available to his publisher.

Meyrink was living in Munich by the beginning of 1907; his son, Harro, was born there in January 1908. The next documentary evidence for his residence in Munich is for the end of 1910; he stayed there until September 1911 at the latest. By then he had moved to Starnberg, a town on Lake Starnberg some fifteen miles to the south of Munich, which was to be his home for the rest of his life.

What happened between 1908 and 1910 is unclear. He certainly travelled widely. There are letters and cards he sent from Lake Garda, the Italian Riviera, Prague, Berlin, the canton of Thurgau in Switzerland (all 1908) and the Mondsee to the east of Salzburg (1910). Some of these journeys sound like holidays, in one case at least (Prague) he claimed to have travelled there on 'family business'. Whether these two years were genuinely a period of no fixed abode, or whether he had a base in Munich, or at least regarded it as such, is impossible to tell. In a letter of 23.3.1907 in the collection in Munich City Library he talked of Lake Starnberg, 'where my wife and I intend to move permanently on 1/X.' It was, however, to be another four years before he carried out the intention expressed there.

If these years were unsettled years domestically, they were
also precarious years financially. In fact Meyrink's financial
situation had been precarious ever since his imprisonment
and the collapse of his bank, maybe even earlier.[11] Perhaps the
sale of his portrait by Kokoschka was part of his attempt
to keep his head above water financially. The fact that the
original payment was in francs suggests the portrait was done
in Switzerland, where Loos had sent Kokoschka to do por-
traits of friends and acquaintances, though Wingler tentatively
dates it as 1910 in Munich.[12] Ursula von Mangoldt recounts
the story as told to her by Meyrink:

> Kokoschka, who was still unknown at the time, came
> to Meyrink one day and said, 'I must paint you.' –
> 'Really?' Meyrink replied. 'If you must, then go ahead.
> How long will it last?' – 'Oh, one hour,' said Kokoschka,
> taking a few tubes out of his pocket and starting to paint.
> After a certain time he called out, 'Finished.' Meyrink
> inspected his portrait and asked, 'Do I really have such a
> long nose?' Kokoschka looks at him, uses his thumb to
> wipe off part of his nose and asks, 'I presume you're
> happy now?' – 'Certainly,' said Meyrink in a serious
> tone, 'what now?' – 'You can keep it.' – 'That's all
> I needed. Thank you very much.' Now Kokoschka

[11] For some details on Meyrink's financial situation in these years, see Lube,
pp. 52–55.

[12] Austria did issue 20 franc gold coins but they were not for general cir-
culation. Perhaps Meyrink was misremembering the precise details of
the story when he told it to Mangoldt many years later. For one rather
grotesque experience Kokoschka had when carrying out the commissions
Loos found for him, see: 'My first journey to Switzerland' in: Oskar
Kokoschka: *Stories from my Life*, tr. Michael Mitchell, Eithne Wilkins and
Ernst Kaiser, Riverside, 1998, pp. 54–58.

named the price. 'How much? Sixty francs? No, sir, I haven't got that much. But I'll give you ten francs.' He handed over the money and hung the portrait in the lavatory. No one would have recognised it as Meyrink.

A few years passed. An art dealer wrote from Frankfurt asking whether the portrait was still available. Meyrink sent a telegram: 'Yes, but not for less that 12,000 marks.' and lo and behold, the Frankfurt dealer actually sent the money.[13]

It was confiscated in 1938 as part of the Nazis' campaign against 'degenerate art'. It has since disappeared, though reproductions are extant.[14]

Obtaining a *salaried* situation with *Simplicissimus* had brought some relief, but it looks as if that ended in 1907–08. There are contributions from him to the magazine for every year from 1901 to 1908, but the enthusiasm of his first two full years as a contributor seems to have waned: in 1901 there was one piece, in 1902–8, 1903–9, 1904–3, 1905–4, 1906–6, 1907–5, 1908–3. There are no more stories by him in *Simplicissimus* until 1914–16, when five of the stories later collected in the volume *Bats* appeared. His contributions to the periodical *März* are also restricted to the years 1907 and 1908.

Both of these magazines were published by Albert Langen. Whether Langen's death in 1909 was, at least in part, the cause of the disappearance of Meyrink from their pages after July 1908 is unknown, but his problems began at least a year earlier. In a letter to Langen of 14.7.1907 he said:

[13] Mangoldt, p. 99.

[14] There is a small black-and-white reproduction in Hans Maria Wingler: *Oskar Kokoschka: The Work of the Painter*, 1958, Salzburg/ London, p. 297. There is a larger, rather blotchy reproduction in Smit, p. 106.

The monthly salary of 400 marks just about made it possible for me to effect a shift in my way of life and burn a few tiresome boats behind me; but if, *just now of all times*, this support were to prove fragile, I would find myself in a truly *terrible* situation. – As for my productivity, I can assure you on my word of honour that my dilatoriness will be a thing of the past this very month.[15]

The implication of this is that his salaried position was threatened with termination. The fact that after that letter only five further pieces by Meyrink appeared in *Simplicissimus* in 1907–08, and no more until 1914, suggests that his appeal was unsuccessful.

The three collections of his stories, published in 1903, 1904 and 1907 had proved fairly popular and would presumably have brought in a little money, but his main hope in improving his finances lay in writing a successful novel. The idea first occurred in 1906, but it was not until 1913/14 that *The Golem* appeared as a serial in a magazine and in 1915 in book form, when it was immensely successful. In the meantime he was compelled to turn to translation to provide a regular income. The first book he translated, which appeared in 1909, was one the subject of which presumably interested him personally: Camille Flammarion, *Die Rätsel des Seelenlebens* (The Mysteries of our Inner Life, 1909). Library catalogues are strangely reticent about the title of the original, but it is probably *L'Inconnu et les problèmes psychiques*, the first edition of which, as well as the English translation (*The Unknown*) was published in 1900. Max Brod says that among the books Meyrink lent him while he was still living in Prague were some by Flammarion.[16]

---

[15] In Munich City Library
[16] Brod, p. 302.

Flammarion was a well-known astronomer who also took a scientific interest in spiritualism. The topics the book covered, as listed in the subtitle, are: manifestations of the dying, apparitions, telepathy, psychic communications, thought transference, clairvoyance, the world of dreams, foretelling the future. The book corresponded very closely, both in subject matter and approach, to Meyrink's own interests, which is presumably why he wrote an introduction to it as well. He also translated the second volume of *The Autobiography of Sir Henry Morton Stanley* (Stanley: *Mein Leben*, 1911).

He then started on the works of Dickens for Albert Langen. This must have occupied his time fairly fully, since between 1909 and 1914 sixteen volumes appeared (*Christmas Stories, David Copperfield* (3 vols.), *Bleak House* (4 vols.), *The Pickwick Papers* (2 vols.), *Nicholas Nickleby* (2 vols.), *Martin Chuzzlewit* (3 vols.), *Oliver Twist*). Even though Dickens was one of his favourite authors from childhood, the fact that he was compelled to devote so much time to this work is an indication of the seriousness of his financial difficulties.

One of his ways of expediting the translation was to use the latest technology. Just as he had been, he claimed, the owner of the first motor car in Prague, so he was most probably the first author in Munich to use a Parlograph, a kind of very early dictaphone. The results, however, were not always as satisfactory as he might have hoped (unless this is just another excuse for his dilatoriness). He wrote to the publishers on 22.7.1914:

> I would *very* much ask you to exercise just a little more patience regarding the MS of volume 18. At the time, the Parlograph rolls were typed out by a temporary typist and are unfortunately so abysmal that I can only use parts – will more or less have to do everything again, a fact which is already making my hair stand on end.

Was his habit of leaving out whole chunks of Dickens's English another way of speeding things up? Could he not be bothered with passages he found awkward or tedious to translate? It is a temptation to which translators are subject. Some reviewers criticised this habit and Langen's editors questioned it. Meyrink justified his cuts as part of his legitimate approach to translation.

Only sixteen of the planned twenty volumes appeared, the rest being abandoned because of poor sales. Mixed reactions from reviewers and readers might be part of the explanation, but another is certainly that there was a glut of Dickens on the German market at the time, at least five publishers bringing out editions in the decade preceding the First World War.

Despite the mixed reception at the time, Meyrink's translation was recently brought back into print. It was highly praised by the writer Arno Schmidt, who called it 'far and away the best German translation' (of Dickens) and the literary magazine *Buchkultur*, said, 'In comparison to others it is more elegant and fresher in its language, revealing what one might call a modern Dickens.' Perhaps the Parlograph helped give Meyrink's Dickens translation a fluency which other, more conscientious ones perhaps, lack. Another factor contributing to the fluency of his translations was presumably his former practice of reading out the Theosophical Society's *Siftings* in German at meetings, which he claimed had given him fluency in extempore translation. And his reward for the work was not only financial – the way the brooding, menacing city of Prague becomes an almost animate presence in *The Golem* seems to owe something to Dickens's London, especially its portrayal in *Bleak House*.

The four plays Meyrink wrote together with Roda Roda between 1909 and 1913 – *Der Sanitätsrat* (The Medical Officer of Health); *Bubi*; *Die Sklavin aus Rhodus* (The Slave from Rhodus); *Die Uhr* (The Clock) – were presumably also a result of his need to make money, rather than any interest in the theatre. This is even hinted at in one of the plays, *The Slave from Rhodes*. The character Diogenes is not the ancient philosopher, but a writer who is deep in debt: Diogenes is a pseudonym and the barrel is his hiding place from his creditors. He bewails the financial situation of the writer: 'You can only live from writing once you're well and truly dead. People only buy the classics . . . So far all I've had from my writing is a succès d'estime and an empty stomach.' (quoted in Qasim, 67)

Roda Roda (the pen name of Sandór von Rosenfeld) was a Hungarian army officer whose first pieces appeared in *Simplicissimus* at the same time as Meyrink's. They met in Vienna, when Meyrink was editor of *Der liebe Augustin* and introduced Roda Roda to the group of writers, including Paul Busson and Peter Altenberg in the Café Imperial. They met again in Munich and collaborated on the four plays, the first three of which were comedies. Roda Roda's speciality was the humorous anecdote and they felt compelled to preface the fourth play with a note: 'Some of our friends assume that Meyrink wrote the serious parts of this play, Roda the comic ones. No. In every line *The Clock* is our joint work.' But there may be more behind this jokey note. Meyrink and Roda Roda wrote separate versions of the play and handed them in to the Hoftheater in Munich without indicating which version was by which author, agreeing to accept the theatre's decision. When Meyrink's was preferred, Roda Roda, who was much more experienced in writing for the theatre and had had considerable success with his comedy *Der Feldherrnhügel* (The Commander's Observation Hill, 1910), was unhappy and demanded what amounted to a recount. Meyrink needed to pour a considerable amount of oil on the troubled waters, of which the note quoted from above was presumably the final drop. Despite the disagreements and irritations that were almost bound to occur in the course of such a collaboration, Roda Roda described Meyrink in his autobiography as:

> A man who, through the wisdom of the Orient and the Occident, had thought his way up into a higher sphere of understanding far removed from reality . . . Later on I wrote four plays with him and every hour with this fine man was a privilege and a delight for me.[17]

The four plays were performed and later published, but with no great success and Meyrink's enthusiasm quickly waned. Even before the first performance of *The Clock* in January 1914, he wrote to Roda Roda (6.5.1913), 'I am so thoroughly fed up with everything to do with the theatre that I can only see *one* solution: Get out,' and in a later letter (30.6.1913) he sighed, 'I wish I already had *this* flop behind me.' He ceded his rights to the play to Roda Roda for 7,000 marks; a similar proposal regarding the other three plays was discussed, though it is not known whether it was carried out.

Munich was the capital of the Kingdom of Bavaria which, in the aftermath of the defeat of the French by the Germans and less than five years after Bavaria itself had been defeated by Prussia in the Austro-Prussian War, had become part of the newly founded German Empire in 1871. In fact it was the King of Bavaria, Ludwig II, who had offered the imperial crown to the unwilling Wilhelm I of Prussia. The motivation for the offer was neither German nationalism nor love of Prussia, but the large sums Bismarck offered Ludwig, who constantly needed money to pay for his grandiose building projects such as Neuschwanstein Castle, out of his 'reptile funds'. Like many Bavarians, Ludwig remained hostile to Prussia, despite an annual 'allowance' of 300,000 marks, saying that he feared the

[17] Roda Roda, *Roman*, p. 534.

Bavarian troops returning from victory over the French might be infected with 'those damned pro-Prussian, sham German ideas.' This antipathy towards Prussia was something Meyrink shared and made him feel at home in the city.

Despite its antipathy to Prussia, Bavaria shared in the rapid economic growth of the Empire which made Germany one of the leading industrial nations of the world by 1900. Munich doubled its population and acquired new industrial districts, often including firms involved in the latest technology. At the same time Munich grew into one of the most important artistic centres in Germany, attracting painters, writers and musicians from Germany and other parts of Europe, for example Ibsen (1875–78 and 1885–91) and Vasily Kandinsky (1896–1914). German painters included Franz von Lenbach and Franz von Stuck, the writers Thomas Mann and, for a while, Rilke, the composers Hans Pfitzner, Max Reger and Richard Strauss. It was also a centre of the avant garde, with the painters of the *Blaue Reiter* group and writers such as Frank Wedekind, the author of *Spring Awakening* and the Lulu plays who also performed in the cabaret *Die Elf Scharfrichter* (The Eleven Executioners).

The opening of Thomas Mann's novella 'Gladius Dei', written 1899–1901, is an evocation of Munich as a city permeated by art. The overture to the story reaches its climax with:

Art is blooming, art holds sway, wielding its rose-wreathed sceptre over the city with a smile. On all sides there is reverent concern that it should flourish, on all sides there is assiduous work devoted to promoting it, an artless cult of line, of ornament, of form, of the senses, of beauty . . . Munich was resplendent.[18]

[18] Thomas Mann: 'Gladius Dei' in: *Frühe Erzählungen 1893–1912*, Frankfurt/Main, 2004, pp. 222–225.

Although Mann's tribute to Munich as the metropolis of art expresses a truth about the city, there is also, as there usually is with Mann, an ironic side to it, just as there was another side to Munich. The indigenous inhabitants were very conservative, their links with traditional values expressed in their dress which retained touches of rural folk costume in the loden coats, the grey loden jackets with green facings, the hats with the tuft of chamois hair, even *lederhosen* and *dirndls*. The city of Renaissance-style architecture and the *Blauer Reiter* was, of course, also the city of the October Beer Festival; the city of the literary/artistic coffee houses, the Café Stefanie, the Café Luitpold, was also the city of the *Hofbräuhaus*, the huge temple to beer; Hitler's first attempt to seize power was in Munich; it is generally referred to as the 'Beer Hall Putsch' from the *Bürgerbräu* where it started.

Meyrink's Munich was the Munich of the coffee house. The coffee house was a key cultural institution throughout Central Europe. Particular ones were the regular, often daily, meeting places of different groups of artists, writers, journalists. An impoverished writer, it was said, could spend hours there over a coffee and a glass of water without being molested by the waiter. Besides newspapers and magazines, many would provide paper and pens for their regulars, some of whom more or less set up house there; the only postal address of Peter Altenberg, the doyen of bohemian Vienna, for example, was his regular coffee house. As Alfred Polgar said of a café, 'It's not a coffee house, but an attitude to life.'[19]

Cafés Meyrink frequented were, among others, the Café Luitpold, where the group included Frank Wedekind and Heinrich Mann, and the Café Stefanie on the corner of Amalienstrasse and Theresienstrasse, where he played chess with the anarchist writer Erich Mühsam; it is also the setting

---

[19] Alfred Polgar: 'Theorie des Café Central' in: *Kleine Schriften*, 4, Reinbek, 1984, p. 254.

for his story 'Wie Dr Hiob Paupersum seiner Tochter rote Rosen brachte' ('How Dr Job Paupersum Brought his Daughter Red Roses', *Latern* 68–81). Perhaps they were even observed by the young Heinrich Himmler and his elder brother, Gebhard, who later wrote in his unpublished 'Reminiscences':

> We sometimes looked in through the windows of Café Stefanie, called 'Café Megalomania' because of the artists from the Schwabing district who went there, and watched the chess players making their moves with earnest expressions on their faces, often with a glass of water before them and a toothpick between their teeth.[20]

About twenty-five years later, in 1933, Meyrink's books were banned by the Nazis under regulations promulgated by the 'Reich Office for Combating Immoral Pictures and Writings' and publicly burned.

Meyrink called Munich 'the city of art with horn buttons'. Munich liked to see itself as the 'city of art'; Meyrink's addition of horn buttons is an allusion to the echoes of folk costume in popular Bavarian dress. His description of the city combines its dual aspect as a centre of 'high' art and a provincial, even philistine environment, which he lampooned as mercilessly as he had the North German variant he found in the writings of Gustav Frenssen. The passage probably also contains a lampoon on Mann's picture of Munich in 'Gladius Dei':

> Munich, the city of art with horn buttons, is in a fever of excitement. The day before yesterday Wedekind was

---

[20] Katrin Himmler: *The Himmler Brothers*, tr. Michael Mitchell, London, 2007, p. 37.

given a good thrashing by the Young Men's Association, Frau Kommerzienrat Zettelhuber rode across the field where the October Beer Festival is held in her new white-sausage gown . . .

And ferment everywhere! Revolution in painting! The leading brushes of the city, it is whispered, have renounced the old school – from now on the radishes on the beer mugs will be painted the other way up, with the root at the top. And a new style of villa with the roof hanging right down over its ears and wooden balconies like shut gobs – à la Cléo de Mérode with motoring goggles.

(*Fledermäuse*, 315–6)[21]

This passage comes in 'Der heimliche Kaiser' (The Secret Emperor), Meyrink's contribution *Der Roman der XII* (The Novel of the XII), a novel consisting of contributions from twelve writers. In Meyrink's chapter the hero's father employs an orang-utan as a servant:

'She wears a *dirndl* when she goes out shopping, that way she doesn't particularly stand out among the female population of Munich. I presented her predecessor, a Frau Huber from Lower Bavaria, to the new zoo – they didn't notice anything special . . .'

(*Fledermäuse*, 320)

And the hero's father, a dead alchemist goes on:

---

[21] 'White sausages' – veal sausages – are a Bavarian speciality, sometimes used as a symbol of the whole area; the German for brush – *Pinsel* – also means 'twit'; long white radishes are a favourite accompaniment to beer in Munich beer gardens; Cléo de Mérode was a dancer who was at least equally celebrated as the epitome of glamour.

'Since I've been dead I've had no problems here in
Munich. The authorities trust me implicitly, since I
never go out without chamois-leather trousers, bare
knees and green woollen calf-warmers.'

(*Fledermäuse*, 323)

Meyrink's most extended satire on Munich is the short
story 'Veronica the Wild Pig', in which the sow, in a home-
made version of folk costume, conquers Munich with a *schuh-
plattler* dance consisting of 'an idiotic pittter-patter on the
boards' accompanied by her shrill squeaks, which is greeted
with thunderous applause and praised as patriotic *Heimatkunst*;
'The sole admirer of Oscar Wilde and Maeterlinck in the city,
a degenerate newcomer from outside, hid in the lavatory,
trembling.' (*Wunderhorn*, 17) Although often translated in
architectural contexts as 'vernacular art', folksy art would be
a more accurate rendition of the term. In his rejection of
Heimatkunst, Meyrink once more agreed with Adolf Loos,
who called it 'faux naïveté', a 'deliberate lowering of standards
to an earlier cultural stage . . . it is time all this childish babble
that goes under the name of *Heimatkunst* stopped.'[22]

As his participation in coffee-house culture indicates,
Meyrink was sociable. In his early years in Prague he was the
centre of a band that enjoyed the nightlife of the city. Later on
he gathered a group of younger artists and writers round him.
In Vienna and Munich he was a frequent attender at the
established literary coffee houses. For Roda Roda he was
'brilliant company;'[23] for Karl Wolfskehl he was a 'grand-
master of conversation'. Wolfskehl, who saw him with his
Parlograph around 1910, goes on:

[22] Loos: *On Architecture*, pp. 114, 117.
[23] Roda Roda, *Prager Tagblatt*, 6.12.1932.

People hung on his lips . . .it is, therefore, understandable that it was in the spoken word that he was completely himself, that even his large-scale works form one single emotional unit, that everything he had published is, in the most non-literary sense of the word, 'storytelling'.

And yet he did not entirely belong, he was in, but not entirely of his surroundings. Those who encountered him in those years frequently suggest his eye, at least his inner eye, was fixed on something beyond his immediate surroundings. Talking of Schwabing, the bohemian quarter of Munich, Karl Wolfskehl said Meyrink 'was only connected with it topographically, and that only for a while.'[24]

[24] Karl Wolfskehl: *Briefe und Aufsätze*, Hamburg, 1966, pp. 200–2.

7

The Golem

The long road to publication

In Prague, even before he started writing for *Simplicissimus*, Meyrink had expressed the intention of writing a novel. Whether it was seriously meant or not and whether he already had any idea of plot or characters is unknown. It is also unknown when he began work on the novel that was to become *The Golem*. Buskirk[1] puts it at 1904, but with very little concrete evidence. The first mention of it is in a letter to Alfred Kubin of 19.1.1907:

> *März* has asked me to pass on a request to you ('without prejudice' as they say) to send a few pictures to go with my *new* novella. It is expected that this novella with your pictures will first appear in *März* and then immediately afterwards as a *single* book. Langen does want to retain the right (which he will certainly not exercise) to *be allowed* to reject one or other of your pictures, if for any reason they don't suit him. Since, however, he always listens to me, that's only a matter of form – anyway, he's sure to like your pictures very much. If you wait a few days I'll send you the first 26 pages of the novella typed out. Anyhow, it would be a good idea to indicate your

[1] Buskirk, p. 26.

willingness to *März straight away*, so that they don't change their mind.[2]

Kubin's essay 'Wie ich illustriere' (How I Illustrate) makes it clear that the 'novella' was the initial version of the novel that was to become *The Golem*. According to Meyrink, the twenty-six pages represented one eighth to one sixth of the expected length. 'Novella' is not a word Meyrink often used for his writings, 'sketch' or 'short story' were his normal designation. In itself it suggests something longer and more complex in composition that his pieces for *Simplicissimus*, but not something as extended as a novel. One hundred and fifty-six *typed* pages is longer than one would expect for a novella; it seems not impossible that Meyrink was influenced by the English word 'novel', especially considering that it would eventually be published 'as a *single* book'; by November 1908 he was referring to it as a novel.

Meyrink's original proposal to Kubin, whom he had known at least since 1904, when the artist supplied some illustrations for *Der liebe Augustin*, was that he should send the artist each chapter as it came off the production line. Kubin was unhappy with this suggestion, however the problem was solved when the production line came to a standstill and no more material arrived from Meyrink; Kubin commented:

> Since in the youthful urgency of those years of development my drawing style was constantly changing, I could not wait for the continuation of the *Golem* and therefore used the completed designs for my own novel, *The Other Side* (which was published in 1909).[3]

As he did with a number of his friends, Meyrink gave

[2] Kubin Archive, Lenbachhaus, Munich.
[3] Alfred Kubin: *Aus meiner Werkstatt*, Munich, 1973, p. 73.

Kubin a brief role in one of his stories. The narrator of 'Die vier Mondbrüder' (The Four Moon Brethren) spends his lonely nights listening to 'the boisterous sounds coming through the surrounding silence from the nearby robber's castle of the wild painter *Kubin*, who holds riotous orgies with his seven sons.' (*Fledermäuse*, 140) Kubin's marriage to Schmitz's sister in fact remained childless.

When Meyrink's novel finally appeared, in 1915, some vignettes were produced as decoration, but Meyrink rejected them. An edition with eight lithographs by Hugo Steiner-Prag was brought out in the same year as the first edition. In 1916 Steiner-Prag added a further seventeen to create a portfolio: *Der Golem. Prager Phantasien* (The Golem. Prague Fantasies) which is considered one of his masterpieces and which is a perfect visual realisation of the novel.[4]

How much Meyrink had added to the original twenty-six pages when he struck what Kubin described as a 'sterile period' is unknown. His repeated assertions that the novel was almost finished are unconvincing. In a letter of 18.11.1908 to Langen, who was presumably pressing him to deliver a different piece of work, he said:

> I beg you to allow me another week. – I am just *finishing off* my novel and cannot break off at the moment – even were I to be granted eternal salvation. I'd lose the thread, perhaps for good. I'll submit the novel to you straight away.[5]

An extract was published in the magazine *Pan* in 1911, with a similar claim that the novel now was in the process of

[4] Reproduced in the Tartarus Press edition of *The Golem*, Carlton in Coverdale, n. d.

[5] Munich City Library; italics MM.

completion. That extract is the third chapter, 'Prague', in the published edition, but the version in the magazine is substantially different.

His contract with the publisher (not Langen, but Kurt Wolff) was concluded in March 1912 with the submission date for the manuscript of 1 February 1913. On 24. 1. 1913 Meyrink's wife wrote to the publishers asking for the first chapters to be returned: 'My husband is now working on the novel again and needs the opening for coherence.' When pressed for the manuscript by Wolff, Meyrink claimed he had come to a verbal agreement with Wolff's partner, Ernst Rowohlt, to postpone delivery until the autumn, at the same time claiming, 'The whole manuscript is complete to the extent that it can be printed *if necessary*; it was in that state when my wife wrote to you recently.' (12.2.1913) Despite Wolff's protests, the novel was not completed until the autumn of that year. The serial publication in the magazine *Die Weissen Blätter* began in September 1913, and continued until February 1914; the book, originally planned for the autumn of 1914, eventually appeared in October 1915. (*Die Weissen Blätter* was an imprint of the Kurt Wolff Verlag and used for serial publication; Kafka's story *Metamorphosis* appeared there in 1915 and then in book form in the same year).

The publishers have added to the confusion surrounding Meyrink's first novel. Ernst Rowohlt founded the company, Ernst Rowohlt Verlag, in 1908, with Kurt Wolff as a sleeping partner. After personal disagreements between them, Wolff took over the company in 1912 and changed it into Kurt Wolff Verlag (the well-known present-day Rowohlt Verlag was founded in 1919). In their memoirs, both Rowohlt and Wolff claimed to have had the first contact with Meyrink. Rowohlt said he had gone to see Meyrink:

Having heard that Gustav Meyrink was writing a novel I went to see him in Starnberg, where he was living at the time in a charming cottage by the lake. He worked high up in a tree, where he'd made a wooden house, to which you had to climb up by a huge ladder. He gave me roughly the first forty pages of *The Golem* to read. I was so delighted by this fragment that I immediately came to an agreement with him for the book. He got an advance which was very high for those days . . .[6]

Meyrink was in Starnberg by September 1911 at the latest, the chapter from *The Golem* in *Pan* appeared that year, the contract was signed in March 1912 and Rowohlt left the company in November of that year. As far as the timing is concerned, Rowohlt's version is possible. Max Brod confirms that Meyrink worked in a kind of tree house, though he is talking about a different villa where he visited Meyrink some years later:

Some time after the success of *Der Golem* I visited Meyrink in his beautiful villa on Lake Starnberg . . . Only one thing recalled his former eccentricities – the study he had built for his work. It was at the other end of the garden from the villa and consisted of one room, but that raised up in the air on stilts. I cannot remember whether you had to climb up to it by a rope ladder or a spiral staircase. Meyrink told me that he not only wrote up there, he also kept various kinds of snakes and lizards and grew the most magnificent cactuses.

(Brod, 305)

Was a tree-house study, or something similar, a regular feature of Meyrink's many homes, or was Rowohlt perhaps

[6] Ernst Rowohlt, quoted in *Ernst Rowohlt in Selbstzeugnissen und Bilddokumenten*, Reinbek bei Hamburg, 1967, p. 41.

remembering the famous House by the Last Lamp, into which Meyrink only moved after *The Golem* had been published. It is one of the details that casts doubt on Rowohlt's version. His partner at the time, Ernst Wolff, wrote in his memoirs:

What or who caused Gustav Meyrink, who lived on Lake Starnberg, to turn up in our offices in Leipzig, I do not know. At that time Meyrink had written nothing apart from short pieces in *Simplicissimus*, which had been published without notable success in book form. As well as that he had translated twenty volumes of Dickens.

I remember Meyrink's visit well: an aristocratic looking gentleman with impeccable manners and a slight limp. He had the honour, he said, of suggesting we take his first novel, which was finished, though not yet typed out. He had spoken it into a dictating machine . . . It would, he went on, be several months before he could send the manuscript of *The Wandering Jew*. He had brought a handwritten copy of the first chapter. He wished to have the contract for the novel signed before he returned to Munich the next day. He did not, he said, require the usual royalties, but an immediate payment of 10,000 marks as a once-and-for-all fee for all rights and all editions in foreign languages. Would I be so good as to read these pages, which he respectfully submitted to my judgment. The unusual suggestion was made in concrete terms and with the utmost seriousness (and I had imagined the author of 'The German Bourgeois' Magic Horn' was a humorist).

Somewhat nonplussed and embarrassed, I read the handwritten folio sheets – which I have kept to this day – and then, having finished, I had to say 'Yes' or 'No' . . . The title of the novel, *The Wandering Jew*, was later changed to *The Golem* and the book sold hundreds of thousands of copies . . .[7]

Wolff's memoirs contain a number of inconsistencies. His correspondence with Meyrink suggests the initial contact was in fact by letter, rather than the dramatic personal visit both he and Rowohlt suggest. The early title of *The Golem* was not 'The Wandering Jew' (which was probably the first title of Meyrink's second novel, *The Green Face*), but 'Der Stein der Tiefe' (The Stone from the Depths), which is how he refers to it in his introduction to the chapter published in *Pan*; at the time Wolff claims Meyrink came to visit him, late 1911 or early 1912, 'The German Bourgeois' Magic Horn' had not yet been published, nor had the Dickens edition reached twenty volumes.

These inconsistencies are probably largely due to the fact that Wolff's memoirs were not published until the 1960s, the distance in time leading to the confusion of dates and books. Meyrink did turn up in Leipzig at some point and perhaps Rowohlt did visit him in Starnberg. What the memoirs of both publishers do confirm is the indelible impression Meyrink made, both in his physical presence and in his personality. However, the letters between Kurt Wolff and Meyrink make it clear that the contact regarding the publication of *The Golem* came from Wolff.[8] The latter wrote in 19.9. 1911 referring to the extract which had just appeared in *Pan* and enquiring whether Meyrink had found a German publisher for the novel. Meyrink's reply six days later is interesting: 'Many thanks for your kind offer. If I decide to have my novel appear in German, which, however, will not happen until one year after the publication of the English edition, I

[7] Wolff, pp. 17–8.
[8] Wolff's correspondence is in Yale University Library,

will not omit to send you my manuscript.' Whether Meyrink took any concrete steps to find an English publisher is unknown. It is more likely to be an expression of his dissatisfaction with German publishing. His intention of finding an English publisher is mentioned in his foreword to the *Pan* extract, the reason given being: 'it annoys me that since Germany has started "reading", works of art are left in a corner to die, while any old Alpine shit is consumed ecstatically.' 'Alpine shit' is, of course, *Heimatkunst*, the folksy art he objected to.

The fact that Meyrink, as Wolff states, demanded and received a – for the time – large one-off payment of 10,000 marks[9] in lieu of royalties and not an 'advance' is confirmed by the contract. Meyrink's unusual procedure of approaching a publisher not only with a manuscript, but also with a peremptory demand was doubtless a result of his permanent financial difficulties. It did not stop him later complaining that he had given away his rights and suggesting he had been cheated by the publishers. 'Publishers and art dealers,' he said in a letter of 17.9.1921, 'are always the same kind of scoundrels.' But Meyrink could be as ruthless as he assumed publishers were. In a letter of 8.2.07 to Kubin he said, 'First of all I'll squeeze all possible concessions out of Rütten und Loening, then bring in Langen and let the best man win . . . Langen cheats in the royalty statements.'[10] Wolff in his memoirs insists that 'despite the one-off payment, the author shared extensively in the profits.'[11]

After the huge success of *The Golem* people tended to assume he must be well off, which was far from the case. By 1921 he was in serious disagreement with Kurt Wolff Verlag,

---

[9] A rough conversion suggests it was the equivalent of £500 in English currency at the time.

[10] Kubin Archiv, Lenbachhaus.

[11] Wolff, p. 18.

who had done much to popularise his novels. His sales had
dropped and his unearned advances had reached around
30,000 marks. He proposed an agreement whereby he would
sign his author's rights over to the publishers in return for
a lump sum. The agreement was signed in January 1921;
by March Meyrink was contesting it on the grounds that
145,000 volumes had been omitted from the publishers'
accounts. The matter became acrimonious and ended up in
court, though the result is not known.

Smit claims, without saying where the information came
from, that when *The Golem* was published in book form in
1915 the original edition was supposed to be 2,000, but some
error led to 20,000 being produced (Smit, 112). It sounds
unlikely, given the high payment Meyrink received, but
whatever the number, they were soon sold out. The book was
an immediate and resounding success; a special forces edition
and the illustrated edition with Hugo Steiner-Prag's lithographs both appeared in the same year; within two years
145,000 copies had been sold. Much of the credit for this goes
to Georg Heinrich Meyer (no relation!), who ran the company while Wolff was away, having joined up on 2 August
1914, the day after Germany declared war on Russia. Meyer
was something of a marketing genius and the advertising
campaign for *The Golem* was unprecedented in German
publishing. The poet Franz Werfel wrote to Meyer:

All you hear and read about just now is the Kurt Wolff
Verlag. Your publicity (especially the newspaper ads) was
the most intensive imaginable. It was the publisher more
than the author who made *The Golem*.[12]

[12] Werfel to Georg Heinrich Meyer of 2.3.1916, quoted in Kurt Wolff:
Briefwechsel, p. 107.

The advertising pillars were also covered in bright red posters for the book. Such a campaign could hardly have been undertaken for an edition of 2,000; Meyer must have been counting on much larger sales. Meyrink himself took a more cynical view of this advertising campaign in a letter of 22.9.1915 to a friend, Johanna Kanoldt:

Out of necessity I have unfortunately been forced to sell – and very cheaply – my royalties (please keep that to yourself), but my interest in the impact of the book is undiminished; now that the whole of the profit goes to the publishers alone, they will naturally move heaven and earth to get publicity for it and if sales are very high, then the market value of my next novel will rise.

(*Latern*, 454)

The composition of The Golem

Meyrink's struggle to get the material of *The Golem* into novel shape is the subject of similar semi-contradictory stories to those of his contact with the publishers. The need to write something that would bring in a substantial sum of money was probably as strong a motivation as the desire to create a large-scale literary work. Up to this point Meyrink had not written anything longer than about ten pages; most of his *Simplicissimus* stories were shorter than that. It is not surprising, then, that he found it difficult to control his material. In the early stages he wrote to Kubin, 'Often I throw a chapter away three or four times.'[13] Max Krell reported that it was an acquaintance called Felix Noeggerath who helped Meyrink clear up the confusion:

[13] Kubin Archive, Lenbachhaus.

Meyrink summoned his friend, the Sinologist [actually specialist in Indian mythology] and mathematician Felix Noeggerath: 'Here are eighty pages of complete nonsense, everything's swimming before my eyes. You're a man of systematic order, you try and put it on a firm foundation.'

Noeggerath unravelled the tangle. He created a kind of star chart. For each character he made a dot with the name beside it. Characters who were interrelated were joined by lines, the way you see on star charts of the heavens, characters who were of no importance for the movement, meaning and atmosphere of the book were marked down for elimination. This process revealed that the list of characters already amounted to 120 names, of which 90 were entirely superfluous.[14]

Lube is rather dubious about this account. It is true, as he suggests, that Krell's chapter on Meyrink is sensationalistic and also wrong on certain facts. However, Noeggerath is the type of person who may well have helped Meyrink. A student based in Munich between 1904 and 1919, he was an important secondary figure in German cultural life during the first half of the 20th century. Walter Benjamin regularly referred to him in his letters as 'the genius' and also called him 'a universal genius', saying, 'he has the most phenomenal knowledge in mathematics, linguistics, the philosophy of religion and any other subject imaginable.' A possible link to Meyrink is Noeggerath's mother, Rufina Noeggerath, who lived in Paris and was a well-known spiritualist. She wrote an account of spiritualism entitled *La survie, sa réalité, sa manifestation, sa*

[14] Max Krell: *Das alles gab es einmal*, Frankfurt/ M, 1961, p. 45.

philosophie, which had an introduction by Camille Flammarion, the author of the first book Meyrink translated.[15]

Another portrayal of Meyrink's difficulties comes from Wilhelm Kelber in an article entitled 'A Visit to Gustav Meyrink's Widow':

> Work on his first and best-known novel, *The Golem*, extended over seven years. At one point Meyrink got stuck. Then his Viennese friend, Friedrich Eckstein, came on a visit . . . Meyrink told his friend that he did not really know how his novel should continue. Eckstein asked for a pencil and a large sheet of paper, drew a kind of chessboard pattern into which he inserted the characters appearing in the completed part of the novel. Then he suggested a series of further chapters by moving the characters around on the sheet, like chessmen. Meyrink accepted the suggestion and proceeded with the work.[16]

Supporting this version is the well-known friendship between Eckstein and Meyrink. More important, perhaps, is the fact that such a chessboard diagram exists for Meyrink's next novel, *The Green Face*, suggesting that he recognised the usefulness of Eckstein's method. Schmid Noerr, an old friend of Meyrink's, also names Eckstein as the one who disentangled the manuscript.[17]

As Lube points out, Meyrink's usual method, if it can be called a 'method', was to go from character (caricature in the

---

[15] For Noeggerath see Gershom Scholem: 'Walter Benjamin und Felix Noeggerath', *Merkur* 35/ 1981, no. 2. Rufina Noeggerath's book was translated into German in 1907 as *Das Fortleben. Beweise. Kundgebungen. Philosophie. Stimmen aus dem Jenseits* – not as *Das Nachleben* as Scholem suggests.

[16] Wilhelm Kelber in: *Christengemeinschaft*, 1956, no. 3, p. 318.

[17] F. A. Schmid Noerr: 'Die Geschichte vom Golem', *Münchner Merkur*, 16.1.1948.

case of many of his short stories) to plot and theme. It is, therefore, not surprising that his first attempt at a novel should develop into a log-jam of characters, and that he should discuss problems and solicit help from friends. Buskirk says that he showed a new opening to the novel to Roda Roda in 1910 and that in 1911 Max Brod helped him with the cabbalistic background to the novel, though Brod does not mention that in his memoirs.

Despite the long gestation and the difficulties of composition, however, *The Golem* remains Meyrink's most popular novel; for many he remains 'the author of *The Golem*'. His difficulties organising his material may even have contributed to its effectiveness, the lack of an omniscient narrator who explains everything and the way some of the chapters follow each other without explicit links adding to the air of mystery that pervades the novel.

This air of Romantic mystery and decay has become associated with Prague. It is an image of Prague to which Meyrink made one of the most significant contributions and which the modern tourist industry exploits to the full. As Ripellino puts it in his own extravagant style:

> In the agitated, spiritistic prose of a Meyrink, Leppin or Perutz a decayed Prague rolls her eyes and twists her mouth into grimaces. She is a centre of mystagogy . . .[18]

As we saw earlier, this Prague had largely become a thing of the past by the time Meyrink wrote his novel. Old Prague had became associated with the German-speaking population and their attachment to the past can be seen as symbolic of their decline from political, economic, social and cultural dominance. This is the Prague whose atmosphere Meyrink evokes so

[18] Angelo Maria Ripellino, *Magic Prague*, tr. David Newton Marinelli, London, 1995, p. 31.

effectively in *The Golem, Walpurgisnacht* and his last novel, *The Angel of the West Window*. It is a spiritual landscape as much as a city of brick and stone, a place where the 'other' world seems to make its presence tangible. Angelo Maria Ripellino's *Magic Prague* is an excellent, if somewhat overblown portrait of this 'Prague of the mind'. This aspect of the novel led one commentator to suggest:

> Meyrink is the better storyteller, the greater stylist than Kafka. Kafka never produced a description of such vividness and suggestiveness than the description of the old houses in the Jewish quarter (and it was the same environment and the same period).[19]

This is certainly true, though it has to be added that Kafka managed to turn a lack of 'style' into a formidable literary instrument.

Central to the Prague of *The Golem* is the Josefstadt, the old Jewish ghetto. In fact, by the end of the century it had largely been pulled down and rebuilt, on the orders of the Czech city council. The Jews had been released from the obligation to live there following the 1848 revolution, and many had indeed moved out. The old tenements were like rabbit warrens, with doors and passageways knocked through from one building to another, then often closed up again or diverted – as in the block where Pernath lives in *The Golem*. Who actually owned what was often difficult to establish and when families, usually the better-off inhabitants, moved out, apartments were frequently left empty – until someone, often criminals and the like attracted by its usefulness as a bolt-hole, moved in. It is perhaps best described in the words of Hugo Steiner-Prag, the artist who illustrated Meyrink's *Golem*:

---

[19] Ernst Stein: *Die Zeit*, 12/11/65.

Old houses in the Prague ghetto

It was picturesque, hazardous and dreary at the same time. It smelled of corruption and misery. The people fitted the setting. But side by side with this misery lived peaceful lower-class people and pious Jews. On Friday evenings one could hear the monotone of prayers mingling with the bickering of whores and the loud tumult of the drunken . . . Around 1895 the demolition was begun. Hundreds of buildings and alleys were destroyed. It was an unbelievable sight . . . but for one who knew this district as it once was, in spite of its seeming ugliness, it remains immortal.[20]

In the novel these dubious aspects of the ghetto appear, for example in the story of Dr Hulbert and his 'regiment' and in Loisitchek's tavern. It was also one of the haunts of the dandy Meyrink's Bohemian crowd in the early 1890s. By the time Meyrink started writing about it in 1906–7, the ghetto which was at least as much a den of thieves and prostitution as home to the Jewish population, had disappeared. There is a powerful evocation of the disreputable side of the ghetto in its last days in Paul Leppin's piece, 'The Ghost of the Jewish Ghetto'[21].

The legend of the Golem is associated with the 16th-century Rabbi Loew from Prague, who is said to have created an artificial man from clay – the golem. The story has been used many times, the best-known version being Paul Wegener's film, the first, lost, version of which was released in 1915. The extant, 1920 version is close to Meyrink in the eerie atmosphere of the city it creates. Wegener's film is often mistakenly referred to as 'the film of Meyrink's novel'. In fact

---

[20] A note by Steiner-Prag accompanying a book of drawings of Prague for his fiancée, quoted in: *Golem! Danger Deliverance and Art*, ed. Emily D. Bilski, New York, 1988, p. 59.

[21] In: Paul Leppin, *The Road to Darkness*, tr. Mike Mitchell, Sawtry, 1997, pp. 145–151.

they are entirely separate pieces. The well-known 1920 version tells the original story of the legend of the golem and its creator, Rabbi Loew. There is an interesting parallel between the now lost 1915 version and Meyrink's in that both are set in the present day, rather than the past, but that is presumably fortuitous

This is perhaps why Meyrink is sometimes mistakenly classified as an Expressionist writer. One can see similarities between Meyrink and the Expressionist *film*: the feeling of *angst* Meyrink evokes and the brooding hostility with which he animates the buildings of the old ghetto are realised on screen in such films as Wegener's *Golem* and Robert Wiene's *The Cabinet of Dr Caligari*. But he is quite different from German Expressionist *literature*, despite occasional parallels such as the use of one-syllable titles for the chapters of *The Golem*. He shared with the Expressionists their rejection of the bourgeoisie and the materialism of the modern world which, like them, he sought to replace with a new or revived spirituality. But the means by which this rejection was expressed were different. Meyrink's comic-grotesque satire and his espousal of the supernatural horror story are a far cry from the abstract characterisation and declamatory rhetoric of Expressionist drama, and his interest in esoteric religious traditions differs from their generalised use of religious symbolism.

The idea of a golem, the creation of an artificial man from earth, originated in mediaeval Jewish commentaries on a seminal Jewish text, the *Sefer Yezirah* (Book of Creation). It was not until some time in the 18th century that it became a legend associated with the historical 16th-century Rabbi Loew, who was said to have made a golem to protect the inhabitants of the ghetto.

Meyrink made only indirect use of this legend in his novel, turning the golem into a ghostly figure that reappears in the ghetto every thirty-three years. It serves a triple function: as a mysterious presence lurking in a room with no door, it

Back alley in the Prague ghetto

embodies the spirit of the the old ghetto: 'There is something abroad in the Jewish quarter, something connected with the golem that never dies.'[22] Secondly, when the hero, Pernath, meets it at various points in the story, he sees it as his double, so that for the hero – an amnesiac – it seems to represent a past which he must reintegrate into his life and then overcome if he is to make spiritual progress. Beyond that, it also has a function in the overall symbolic structure. The novel has a threefold spiritual hierarchy, as explained by Pernath's guide, the Jewish archivist Shemaiah Hillel: 'It is only things from the realm of ghosts – *kishuf* – that frighten men; life itches and burns like a hair-shirt, but the rays of the sun from the spiritual world are mild and warming.' (*Golem*, 82) In this spiritual hierarchy, the golem appears to represent the realm of ghosts, which is opposed on the one hand to the material world (the 'hair-shirt' of life) and on the other to the state of true spiritual enlightenment, towards which Pernath is led.

In *The Golem*, Meyrink uses material from a number of esoteric traditions, including for example the 'mystical union' of alchemy, but the most important of them is the Jewish Cabbala, especially in the figure and teachings of the Jewish archivist, Hillel. The Hebrew scholar, Gershom Scholem, called Meyrink's use of this tradition 'pseudo-Cabbala',[23] but that does not impinge on its effectiveness as a symbolic structure for a powerful work of fiction, as Scholem himself admits. Meyrink adds a visual component by associating it with the cards of the Tarot pack, which Hillel calls 'a book which contains the whole of the Cabbala.' (*Golem*, 119)

[22] Gustav Meyrink: *Der Golem*, tr. Mike Mitchell, Sawtry, 1995, p. 56.
[23] Gershom Scholem, *From Berlin to Jerusalem*, New York, 1988, p. 133.

8

The First World War

The anti-Meyrink campaign

The success of *The Golem* did not bring Meyrink the great wealth some assumed it must have, but it did bring fame and, in some cases, unwelcome notoriety. As we have already seen, Meyrink fled Vienna because his satires on the military had led to prosecution and a jail sentence. The publication of the three volume edition of his collected short stories, 'The German Bourgeois' Magic Horn', in 1913, was greeted enthusiastically by his supporters:

> Who would have imagined it. Meyrink, our Gustav Meyrink in three volumes. In a nice slipcase and *Collected Works*. We're getting old.
>
> Yes, now the schoolboys will have to study him in their readers, and I can already hear my little granddaughter laboriously and expressively spelling out the words . . .
>
> And we will read again the things that stirred us up all those years ago, not in the same way, however, but with affection, wallowing in our memories . . . [1]

The memories of the authorities in Vienna, sharpened by the war, were less affectionate. In December 1916 the official *Wiener Zeitung* announced:

[1] Kurt Tucholsky: *Gesammelte Werke 1*, Reinbek, 1960, p. 165.

In the name of His Majesty the Emperor! In its decision of 28 Nov. 1916 Pr. XXXV 6216 the Imperial-Royal District Court in Vienna has forbidden the further distribution of the publication by Gustav Meyrink 'The German Bourgeois' Magic Horn' . . . under article IV of the law of 17 December 1862.

(quoted in Qasim, 186)

The atmosphere had changed immediately the war broke out. The enthusiasm that swept Germany, as it did other countries, led even satirical magazines such as *Simplicissimus* to forego criticism and become, essentially, mouthpieces for patriotic propaganda. As the war dragged on and conditions in Germany worsened, calls from right-wing nationalists that everyone pull together increased. Attacks on those regarded as unGerman were one way of arousing popular patriotic fervour and Meyrink, presumably because *The Golem* had made his name known to a much wider audience than his *Simplicissimus* stories, became the target of one such virulent campaign.

It began with an article by an Albert Zimmermann in the June 1917 edition of a periodical called *Bühne und Welt*, which afterwards made its nationalist leanings clear when it became *Deutsches Volkstum*, ie German Nationhood. The article was later also published as a pamphlet. In it Zimmermann discussed the stories in 'The German Bourgeois' Magic Horn' without making it clear, perhaps even initially without being aware, that they had first been published between nine and sixteen years previously, when conditions were very different. His general line was an attack on Meyrink's lack of patriotic feeling:

Meyrink's attitude is not internationalist but *anti-nationalist*. All expressions of nationalism are an abomination to him. He attacks all the nation's endeavours with

156

his characteristic ruthlessness and the favourite objects of his ridicule are the established representatives of our state and nation. The main or secondary aim of all his numerous short stories is to mock the monarchy, officers, representatives of the German nation abroad, in short anything German.[2]

It is perhaps not surprising that during the war Meyrink's satire on the military 'mind', which had aroused the displeasure of the Austrian authorities in peacetime, should bring accusations of a lack of patriotic feeling. However, it was another aspect of his satire that aroused Zimmermann's greatest ire. This was reserved for a passage from the story 'The Ring of Saturn'. It is incidental to the main thrust of the story, which is a grotesque satire on certain adepts of the occult who are trying to isolate the soul. For his experiment the 'master' needed to kill a human being to examine its soul and for that purpose he sought 'some truly useless individual'. Naturally – this is a Meyrink story – he first searched among 'lawyers, doctors, soldiers' but does not find quite what he is looking for. Then he comes upon a whole species of useless beings:

Then came a moment when at last I found what I was looking for. But it was not an individual: it was a whole group.

It was like uncovering an army of woodlice, sheltering underneath an old pot in the cellar.

Clergywives!

The very thing!

I spied on a whole gaggle of clergywives, watching them as they busied themselves about their 'good

[2] Albert Zimmermann: 'Gustav Meyrink', *Bühne und Welt*, 1917, part 4, pp. 161–7.

works', holding meetings in support of the 'education of the benighted classes' or knitting horrible warm stockings and Protestant cotton gloves to aid the modesty of poor little piccaninnies, who might otherwise enjoy their God-given nakedness . . .

And then when I saw that they were about to hatch out new schemes for yet more missionary societies, and to water down the mysteries of the scriptures with the scourings of their 'moral' sewage, the cup of my fury ran over at last.

One of them, a real flax-blonde 'German' thing – in fact a genuine outgrowth of the rural Slavonic underbrush – was all ready for the chop when I realised that she was – 'great with child' – and Moses' old law obliged me to desist.

I caught another one – ten more – a hundred – and every one of them was in the same interesting condition!

So I put myself on the alert day and night, always ready to pounce, and at the last moment I managed to lay my hands on one just at the right moment as she was coming out of the maternity ward.

A real silky Saxon pussy that was, with great big blue goose-eyes.

(*Opal*, 125–6)

'Truly,' Zimmermann exclaimed in horror, 'one does not have to be a fanatic to feel such diabolical mockery of German women as a slap in the face.' The key to Zimmermann's argument and to the furore it caused was the rhetorical question with which he concluded: should one take that from a foreigner, for 'Meyrink's real name is Meyer and he comes from Vienna.' The implication of this was that Meyrink was Jewish, Meyer being a common Jewish name, though it is just as common for non-Jewish Germans. The further implication was that Meyrink was not just a 'foreigner' (exploiting the fact that he was born in Vienna, though he was, of course, a citizen of Bavaria and, by that, Germany) but was by his very nature and origin alien to 'Germanness'. This was made clear in a second pamphlet entitled *Gustav Meyrink und seine Freunde* (Meyrink and his Friends):

> Meyrink's character is specifically Jewish. The management of the important German newspapers is mostly Jewish, the critics are Jewish, as are many literary periodicals. It is hardly surprising that praise of Meyrink soon resounded from all sides.[3]

Being Jewish for these German nationalists was not a simple matter of race or religion, it was a matter of character and attitude. Adolf Bartels, a right-wing nationalist who was an early member of the National Socialist Party, joining in 1925, said in his three-volume *Deutsche Dichtung der Gegenwart* (German Literature of the Present): 'Meyrink has denied he is Jewish, however from his literary physiognomy and the slant of his writings he is Jewish.'[4] This was an accusation which was commonly directed by right-wing nationalists against authors and artists they regarded as critical or 'decadent'.

Zimmermann's attack sparked off a furore and was taken up by many newspapers and magazines. Meyrink's local paper, the *Starnberger Zeitung* of 18.6.1917, regretted the way 'the German author, Gustav Meyrink, who unfortunately lives here in Starnberg, drags German women through the mud,' adding: 'Meyrink's *Golem* is set in the Prague ghetto; he himself is a Jew. What would people say if, for example, a Catholic should write such offensive things about Protestant pastors' wives?'

---

[3] Albert Zimmermann: *Gustav Meyrink und seine Freunde*, Hamburg, n. d. (1917), p.21.
[4] Adolf Bartels: *Die Jüngsten*, a separate edition of the final volume of *Deutsche Dichtung der Gegenwart*, Leipzig, 1921, p. 101.

Although it was the collected edition of Meyrink's short stories that had aroused Zimmermann's initial anger, the attacks quickly spread to *The Golem*, as the quotation from the Starnberg newspaper above indicates, and his next novel, *The Green Face*, which came out in 1916. Both had an important Jewish element, which was used to support the argument that Meyrink was Jewish. The, for those times, unusual advertising campaign, which had contributed to the success of Meyrink's first novel, was used to suggest it was a confidence trick pulled on a German public desperately in need of diversion during the war.

The debate was not entirely one-sided. Some writers came to Meyrink's defence. The *Schutzverband deutscher Schriftsteller* (Association of German Authors) issued a statement protesting against the 'virulent abuse' directed for weeks at Meyrink by certain newspapers which:

> going back to his satirical stories published twelve years ago, try to arouse the impression he 'made diabolical mockery of German women' and spread a 'stench of decay'. At the same time the regularly occurring claim that Meyrink is Jewish – he is neither Jewish nor descended from Jews – seems designed to set off an anti-Semitic campaign against him.'[5]

Signed by writers such as Heinrich Mann and Frank Wedekind, not to mention a genuine 'clergywife', this had little effect. If anything, it added fuel to the fire. The conservative Fichte-Gesellschaft (Fichte Society), which published Zimmermann's pamphlet, replied with a 'counter-statement' and one magazine responded with:

---

[5] Published in a number of papers, e.g. *Stimmen der Zeit*, 1918, no. 1/2, p. 8, or *Das litterarische Echo*, 15.8.1917, column 1418.

We agree with the attacks on the currently fashionable author Gustav Meyrink and regret that in the third year of the war there are still people in Germany who dare to denigrate the absolutely justified struggle against a calculating mocker as 'low personal attacks', 'abuse', and 'anti-Semitic campaign'.[6]

In her PhD thesis Amanda Boyd insists that none of the previous studies 'correctly underscore [sic] the severity of the event for Meyrink's life',[7] but there is relatively little evidence to show precisely how 'severe' the effect was. It certainly did very quickly affect his personal life in Starnberg. There were reports that he and his family were refused service in some local shops and cafés, and, as he pointed out in a letter to Siegfried Jacobsohn, the editor of *Die Schaubühne*:

The Teutomanes' rabble-rousing campaign knows no bounds. For example the *Starnberger Land- und Seebote* published an article attacking me in such personal terms, that the day before yesterday some navvies threw stones at me in the open street. A protest in my favour, sent to the paper by everyone of note in Starnberg, including Bernstorff, was rejected by the editor.[8]

He certainly believed it had affected sales of his novels, which was a serious consideration given his permanently precarious financial state, and it is possible the confiscation of his works by the Austrian authorities in January 1918 was connected with Zimmermann's campaign against him.

[6] *Das litterarische Echo*, 15.10.1917, column 125.
[7] Amanda Charitina Boyd: *Demonizing Esotericism*, PhD thesis, Amherst, 2005, p.169, footnote.
[8] Letter to Siegfried Jacobsohn, the editor of *Die Schaubühne*, quoted in the edition of 19. 7. 1917 (vol. 13, no. 29) p.71.

His initial reaction was one of fury tempered by sarcasm. The passage quoted by Zimmermann, he said, 'had been arbitrarily torn out of context by pan-German jingoists,' adding that he intended 'to tear out one of the bison horns of this and other professional Teutons.' ('Tally-ho', Jacobsohn commented.)[9] Perhaps he regarded the declaration by the *Schutzverband deutscher Schriftsteller* as a sufficient public justification. His one other recorded direct comment on Zimmermann, in a letter of 16.8.1917, is scornfully dismissive:

> I was delighted to read what you wrote about the campaign against me in your story; in the meantime it has assumed quite grotesque forms. At first it was a kind of anti-Semitic smear campaign, but now that the gentlemen realise I'm not Jewish they don't quite know what to say. The main instigator is an ass called Albert Zimmermann from Hamburg.

The debate continued into 1918, but soon the Germans had more serious matters such as defeat and revolution to occupy their minds. The affair rumbled on through the 1920s, however, as Meyrink continued in his attempt to get Bartels to remove the offending statement that he was Jewish from his history of contemporary literature. It was presumably not simply being identified as Jewish that irritated Meyrink – as can be seen from his novels, he had nothing against Jews as such – but the fact that the context in which the 'accusation' was put was entirely negative. Bartels connects 'Judaisation' with 'collapse' and makes statements such as:

That a Jew cannot become a German author,[10] and that a

---

[9] Ibid.

[10] The German word used: *Dichter* has almost bardic connotations it is impossible to give in English.

German author who consorts with Jews [this was directed against Thomas Mann among others] loses what
is best in himself, is a matter of established fact for such
simple folk as we German nationalists are.

. . .

One can say that all Jewish writers unconsciously
distort German life.[11]

Meyrink continued to pursue Bartels through the 1920s
and eventually the matter came to court. He assembled a thick
file of material in support of his case for compensation for the
loss of income he claimed he had sustained through the false
statement that he was Jewish. He collected sales figures for his
books throughout the 1920s from as many publishers as he
could think of (Dürr und Weber, Langen, Reclam, Rikola,
Scherl, Schünemann, Ullstein, Wolff) and statements from
individuals and organisations such as the 'Association for
Combating Anti-Semitism' or the 'Central Association of
German Citizens of Jewish Faith'. One publisher reported a
statement from a bookseller that if he put books by Meyrink
in his window regular customers complained they would take
their custom elsewhere. Final judgment was delivered in the
last year of his life: Bartels was required to correct the statement that Meyrink was Jewish, but his claim for loss of
income was rejected.

There was certainly an obsessive streak in Meyrink's make-
up. In some contexts it can be seen positively as determination, as in his rowing achievements – every elite sportsman
needs an obsessive streak – but going out more often and
rowing more miles than anyone else in the club at the age of
48 perhaps suggests a refusal to accept what others would
regard as reasonable moderation. The same is true of his

[11] Bartels, pp. 89, 92.

researches into the occult. Once he had become convinced of its importance, he was singleminded in his search for evidence. But his experience with the guru Brother Johannes reveals the same reluctance to admit his efforts were leading nowhere when he continued practising his exercises 'for thirteen years with no result whatsoever'. In the duel case he continued to pursue Dr Bauer and the two officers from the honour court when it must have been clear to anyone who took a con-sidered view that he was just making things worse for himself. His detailed depositions come across as obsessive, especially in the frequent underlining. In the case of his complaint against Bartels, he spent almost a decade trying to get one sentence in a large, three-volume work changed. If the cash-strapped writer was hoping for compensation, he must have had a capacity to deceive himself which he had avoided in his investigations into spiritualist phenomena thirty years previ-ously. The increasing anti-semitism of the 1920s was almost certainly one factor in the falling-off of sales of his books, but only one factor. And the claim that Meyrink was Jewish had been made so often that it would be impossible to prove the losses were due solely to Bartels' more academic tome. Despite his denials, the assumption that he was Jewish was widespread. There is a letter from the *Völkischer Beobachter* of 1920 stating that they had corrected the claim that he was Jewish. An article in the illustrated supplement of the same newspaper in 1927 writes, under the heading 'Jewish Eroti-cism': '. . .just like the plagiarist Gustav Meyrink, for example, the well-known depicter of erotic excesses in *The Golem*.'

His Attitude to the War

Zimmermann was correct to call Meyrink antinationalist. Many, especially today, would see that as a matter for praise rather than vituperation, but things were different in the third year of a war that was beginning to go badly for Germany. And Meyrink was particularly allergic to the specific form of nationalism in the German Empire, as was seen in his story 'Wetherglobin'.

But Meyrink's scorn was not really directed at Germany and the Germans as such but at the arrogance of certain parts of German society, especially the military, that served as icons of German patriotism. In his unfinished novel *Das Haus des Alchimisten* (The Alchemist's House), on which he was working towards the end of his life, the main character, Dr Steen, half English, half Mongol, is similarly scornful about the English. When told that one of his theories is rejected by Englishmen, he replies:

> 'By Englishmen? Don't you mean English women?'
> 'How do you mean?'
> 'Because they instinctively sense that they would have to look a little more closely at their Liberty-silk views of the dear Lord, if they were to think the matter through. – That doesn't suit them because it might lead to their approving of the most outrageous atrocities, for example being allowed to play cards on Sundays, the mornings of which should be reserved for prayer, the afternoons for procreation. – And to think something through? For heaven's sake, what would happen to the sacrosanct tradition of narrow-mindedness!'

> (*Latern*, 108)

These are obviously not necessarily Meyrink's views, though the style does echo the sharp irony of the *Simplicissimus* stories, but Steen's partial retraction later on probably does come close to what Meyrink thought, both when he was working on the novel and during the war, over ten years earlier. Steen's half-sister, who is fully English, asks, with an echo of wartime propaganda:

'Since when have you felt you were German? What you are expressing is clearly German hatred. Is not your hope that England is on the wane not the pious hope of the Germans? . . . May God punish England, oh yes,' she added scornfully.

[Steen] 'What are the Germans to me? I don't hate them and I don't love them. I don't hate the English, either, though it might sound like that to you. What I hate is this hypocritical white rabble, whichever nation they claim to belong to. Please don't interrupt. I know what you're going to say. You think Asians are no better than the whites. Of course they aren't. But the Asian soul is ready to ignite; the European soul is burnt out . . .'

(*Latern*, 121–2)

Meyrink's lack of 'primary patriotic frenzy', of which Zimmermann's outpourings are a good example, does not mean that he was anti-German and supported the Entente powers. Belgians fleeing the German invasion brought stories of German atrocities committed by the barbaric 'Huns' which were widely believed and publicised in the West. As a counter to this propaganda campaign German writers published an *Aufruf zur Würde* (Appeal for Dignity), which Meyrink was quite happy to sign.

The appeal began:

The fight for the Germans' position in the world and for their culture, which has been forced upon us, has led, in the foreign press, to a campaign of lies and calumny which has become an immense danger for the public opinion of all civilised nations. The punishment of Louvain and the bombardment of the cathedral of Rheims in particular, which were bitter necessities of war, were taken as an opportunity by foreign writers,

scholars and artists to denigrate the Germans and their
army as a horde of Barbarians and Huns.

The aim of this is to deprive the sacred struggle of
German arms against the allied Russians, English, French,
and Japanese of its justification and dignity.[12]

The 'Appeal' concludes by describing the Allies' 'false
witness' as a 'sin against the spirit of our fight'. Meyrink
signed the 'Appeal', even though it was couched in terms
which he would have satirised mercilessly a few years earlier.
Thomas Mann, whose views, expressed in his *Gedanken im
Kriege* (Thoughts During the War), for example, came very
close to the nationalist insistence on the war as a legitimate
struggle of German 'culture', refused to sign it. His refusal,
however, was not a rejection, more an odd combination of
aloof distaste for the whole business and an understanding of what led the Allies to undertake this propaganda
campaign:

> For a few days I hesitated. I find it absurd that we
> should even bother to defend ourselves against the
> accusation that we are 'barbarians' . . . To urge France
> to show dignity at this moment would be asking too
> much . . . one does not protest against things that are
> said under the impact of severe suffering. What their
> leading intellectuals are saying about Germany at the
> moment is so deranged . . . that it is with a shock that
> we realise that the brain of this people can no longer
> bear the war.[13]

Meyrink, the famous anti-militarist, signed the 'Appeal'

---

[12] A copy with Meyrink's signature is in Munich City Library.
[13] Thomas Mann: *Essays II 1914–1926*, Frankfurt/M, 2002, p. 51.

VIVO: THE LIFE OF GUSTAV MEYRINK

that Mann felt was beneath his 'dignity'. Why? The reason was presumably his anger at the Entente propaganda. He satirised it, for example, in his story 'How Dr Job Paupersum Took Red Roses to his Daughter'. Paupersum, an impoverished – as his name suggests – scientist, has discovered that the deformities of the inhabitants of a Tyrolean village are caused by a virus in the nearby spring water. An 'impresario for monstrosities' comes to visit him in order to exploit his discovery. As an example of what he does, the impresario describes an old man born without arms and legs whom he is going to show to the Queen of Italy as 'a Belgian infant mutilated by German generals', adding that he will say the infant looks so old because he aged rapidly 'through having to watch his mother eaten alive by a Prussian Uhlan.' The impresario proposes that Paupersum should use the virus to create deformities in himself; he would then smuggle him to Paris and exhibit him as 'a guaranteed genuine German professor'. When Paupersum timidly asks what will happen if the war should come to an end in the meanwhile, the impresario replies, 'No need to worry, Herr Doktor, the time when a Frenchman will not believe anything that speaks against the Germans will never come. Not in a thousand years.' (*Fledermäuse*, 77–8)

When the accusations came from the East, rather than the West, Meyrink was able to adopt a similar, though more humorous, aloof attitude as Thomas Mann. In a letter of 2. 4. 15 to Korfiz Holm, one of the *Simplicissimus* editors, he starts by making jokey references to Holm's Russian background, then downplays the Russian propaganda:

The things about 'rape' we hear are certainly seen in the wrong light. Anyone who knows the Russian soul clearly senses behind that kind of thing the excess of selfless gallantry, which expresses itself at every opportunity they have to assure others that the Russians can match the French, their allies, the descendants of Louis XIV, in everything.[14]

A more bizarre and mysterious expression of Meyrink's willingness to 'do his bit' for the war effort was in his relations with officials of the German Foreign Office, from which one telegram and five letters have survived in the archives. Three are from a Legionsrat von Hahn, who since October 1917 had been head of the central office of which the *Nachrichten-abteilung* (Press and Propaganda Department) of the German Foreign Office, from which the letters came, formed part. The letters are from Section B of the Press and Propaganda Department, which distributed printed matter abroad, books and pamphlets as well as pictures and films, though more in neutral than enemy countries.

The first letter, of April 1918, indicates that Meyrink was working on a novel, which the Department was presumably interested in for propaganda purposes, concerning Free-masonry (the telegram has handwritten notes on the back which include the expression 'Freemasonry novel'):

Herewith I am sending you a book which may be of interest to you for your book. These prize essays of the Grand Lodge of Germany certainly show how German Freemasonry occupies itself with vague utopias com-pletely devoid of knowledge of human nature and the world, and of political instinct, while French and English Freemasonry goes about political tasks with cool calculation.

A letter of August announces that the writer is coming to Munich and 'a short exchange of views face to face will

[14] Munich City Library.

presumably help to expedite the matter'. However, the Foreign Office experienced the same difficulties with Meyrink as Kurt Wolff had with *The Golem*: 'I repeat the request I made before that you should complete the novel very soon, for I fear that otherwise time will take the wind out of your sails. Time was very close to 'taking the wind out of Meyrink's sails' when the letter was written: 11 October 1918.

Ursula von Mangoldt said in her memoirs that it was 'at the beginning of the war' that Meyrink had been commissioned by the German Foreign Office to write a book about the role of the Freemasons in the outbreak of war. There is nothing in the archives to support or contradict this dating. Von Mangoldt's version ends with a typical Meyrink incident: he had been sent a box of materials for his novel. Not being able to use it immediately, he put it away; when, after the war, he went to find it, it had disappeared without trace. Had it been secretly removed by the Freemasons?[15] It is a pity to spoil a good story, but for once there is material in the archives that sounds relevant. A telegram from the Foreign Office Press and Propaganda Department of August 1917 says the the press archives urgently needed the Freemasonry material returned. A year later his contact at the Foreign Office asked why the material had been returned, he could send it again if Meyrink wished. Had Meyrink simply forgotten and immediately assumed 'mysterious forces in the service of the Freemasons' were up to their usual underhand tricks?

A letter of August 1918 from an Emil Lessel, who is described in the list of correspondents as a 'diplomat', also discusses another project submitted by Meyrink: a film. It was to use ridicule to combat Lord Northcliffe's propaganda. (Would it have been a predecessor of Chaplin's *The Great Dictator*?) That would, Lessel said, 'be the only effective way of

[15] Mangoldt, pp. 97–8.

combating Northcliffe's campaign of lies, there could be nothing more stupid than to deal with those disgraceful dirty tricks through serious academic discussion.' He was however, doubtful whether the German Foreign Office would be willing to 'don the cap and bells' to prick the balloon of Northcliffe's base lies with the sharp edge of wit.

Reflecting on how to proceed with this project, Lessel continues:

> I consider Hintze the man who would be very sympathetic to precisely this kind of thing, and one would be doing him a favour, as well as furthering the cause, if one could use this weapon to eliminate his current entourage. How about it?

Admiral von Hintze had been appointed foreign Minister in July 1918, which meant that with his proposals Meyrink was coming into close, if indirect, contact with the higher reaches of the German government. That Hintze would approve of countering English propaganda with humour is understandable. Unclear, on the other hand, is the reference to internal politics in the suggestion that the same tactics be used against 'his current entourage'. Hintze was an aristocratic naval officer who had gone into the diplomatic service in 1911. He was a surprise appointment as foreign minister in July 1918, as he had no political experience whatsoever, but by that time the country was effectively ruled by the generals Hindenburg and Ludendorf, so he would presumably have been their appointee. Hintze, however, showed a surprising degree of independence and urged the Kaiser to liberalise the political system. Exactly where Meyrink fitted into this situation is unclear. The most likely explanation seems to be that he is being invited by Lessel to use his well-known ability as a satirist against one side or the other in the debate about how Germany should proceed in the worsening situation.

An earlier letter of June 1918 from an official attached to the civilian administration of Flanders muddies the waters yet again. In conspiratorial tones it talks of 'the matter in question' and suggests a post might be found for Meyrink in the Civilian Administration in Flanders for some secret task:

> Since, however, the Civilian Administration would have to state its reasons in approaching the Foreign Office to have you appointed here and since these reasons would touch on highly confidential matters, I made the suggestion, which was approved, that you yourself should apply to the Foreign Office to be attached to the Civilian Administration.

The writer's recommendation that Meyrink should give as his reason 'an information-gathering trip to Belgium for the purpose of making films' suggests that Meyrink's proposed film, if it did in fact exist (Meyrink did produce outlines for films), was being used as a pretext to conceal something more cloak-and-dagger ('highly confidential matters'), but there is unfortunately no hint as to what that might be.

It is unclear whether Meyrink was approached by someone from the Books and Pamphlets Section of the Foreign Office Press and Propaganda Department, whether a third party was involved or whether Meyrink made the proposal himself. What it does demonstrate is that he was not unwilling to do something for the 'war effort'. His motivation is also unclear. That he became involved out of pure patriotism is very unlikely. The probability is that it was a combination of the desire to produce something that would be published (and paid for), and his distaste for Northcliffe's 'campaign of lies'. This is the only known occasion when Meyrink took an active part in public events. Was there an aspect to his life which was so covert as to be invisible today or, as seems more likely, did the increasingly desperate situation of Germany after the failure of the spring offensive in 1918 mean Meyrink was merely one straw at which officials were clutching?

Germany was devastated by the war, both materially and psychologically. However, the material deprivation it caused did not really start until the 'starvation winter' of 1916–1917 and the psychological effects did not arrive until late in 1918. The German nation had been led to believe that its army was winning and the effect of the sudden revelation of the true situation in September 1918 was traumatic.

Meyrink seems to have taken a more pessimistic view much earlier. In a letter to Johanna Kanoldt of 2.7.1915 he says:

> Recently I was told by a *well*-informed source that unfortunately things look pretty bad for us – Germany; unless there's a miracle, there is no hope of a conclusive victory, for he said we hadn't sufficient troops to advance much further into Russia; in the near future we would have to settle for a defensive strategy à la Flanders which meant the war could last another 2–3 years until all parts have been annihilated. A nice prospect![16]

His source must have been very well-informed. In the middle of 1915 Germany still seemed to be advancing on a tide of victories. The information that the initial defeat of the Russian forces in East Prussia was not decisive and that the military leadership felt they had not enough troops for a push further into Russia must have come from very high up. Was Meyrink already in contact with the higher reaches of the German Foreign Office, or had he been talking to one of the young intellectuals, who were the greatest fans of his

---

[16] Munich City Library.

early satires, and who now occupied senior positions in the administration? The news would fit in with Meyrink's attitude. He does not appear to have shared the wild enthusiasm and triumphalism that seized the country – and most other countries involved – at the outbreak of the war: the trains taking troops to the Western front were covered in chalk inscriptions such as 'Free excursion to Paris'. From very early on he viewed the war in apocalyptic terms as an orgy of destruction – the self-destruction of Europe.

His novel *The Green Face* was published in 1916, though he had probably been working on it since about 1910. It is set in Amsterdam, at some future date when the war has just finished, and is a prophetic vision of a continent exhausted by war. His sharp satirist's eye even seems to foresee the peace conference that will follow:

> Special trains were arriving hourly at the Hague, filled with stony-broke or stony-hearted politicians of all races who were determined to say their immortal piece at the permanent peace conference which was discussing the securest way to bar the stable door now the horse had bolted for good.
>
> (*Green Face*, 16)

The story 'Das Grillenspiel' (Cricket Magic) from the collection *Bats* first appeared in *Simplicissimus* in September 1915. It gives a fantastic account of the outbreak of the war: it is summer 1914 and a German entomologist is travelling round Tibet collecting unknown species of insects. He hears of a Dugpa, 'a priest of the devil . . . a *samtscheh mitschebat*, that is a being that can no longer be described as human, that can 'bind and loose', a being for whom nothing on earth is impossible because of its ability to see time and space as the illusions they are.' (*Fledermäuse*, 55) The scientist, with the kind of superior curiosity typical of Europeans faced with what seem to them amusingly odd native beliefs, expresses the wish to meet the dugpa. It is granted, on condition that he assumes responsibility for anything that happens. They sit beside a little mound that the dugpa asks the European to cover with a white cloth; all he has is an old, faded map of Europe, which he uses. The Tibetan asks if he would like to see cricket magic.

I nodded. It was immediately clear to me what would come – insects would be lured out by whistling or something similar.

I was not mistaken. With a little silver bell they keep hidden about their person, the Dugpa made a soft, metallic chirping noise and immediately a multitude of crickets came out of their hiding holes in the ground and crept onto the white map.

More and more.

Countless insects.

. . .

Suddenly a rainbow patch of light from a prism the dugpa was holding up to the sun fell on the map and a few seconds later the peaceable crickets had turned into a mass of insect bodies tearing each other apart in the most horrible way . . . The buzzing of the hundreds of thousands of wings made a high, whistling noise that went right through me, a screeching combining such fiendish hatred and terrible mortal agony that I will never forget it.

Thick, greenish fluid oozed out from under the heap.

. . .

I could not get the words 'he can bind and loose' out of my mind, gradually they took on fearful form inside my brain: in my imagination the twitching mass of crickets was transformed into millions of dying soldiers.

(*Fledermäuse*, 63–5)

This is presumably meant symbolically, it is almost an allegory of the Europeans arrogantly setting in motion the events that will kill millions and destroy the old social order. However, the idea that such cataclysmic events are caused by occult forces occurs frequently in Meyrink. In another story from *Bats*, 'The Four Moon Brethren', the narrator comments at the outbreak of war:

> I could not wholeheartedly join in the curses the villagers hurled at the enemy states; it seemed to me that the cause behind it was the dark influence of certain natural forces filled with hatred which use human beings like puppets.
>
> (*Latern*, 131)

In the unfinished novel *The Alchemist's House*, when Dr Steen's sister says, 'Nor can I agree with your view that Bolshevism and other great movements of recent years do not have their origin in men themselves but −' and Steen finishes the sentence with, 'but in a realm of − "ghosts".' (*Latern*, 107–8) This is echoed in *Walpurgisnacht* (published 1917) where the vision of the Manchu warns Halberd that a 'cosmic Walpurgisnacht' in which 'ghosts are released' is about to happen. (*Walpurgisnacht*, 86)

The idea also appears in a later essay, 'Dämonenfang in Tibet' (Hunting Demons in Tibet), which appeared in 1931:

> Years ago an Estonian railway engineer who had lived for many years in the East during the time of the last Tsar and had spent much time talking with lamas, assured me that there was no doubt in Russian and Asiatic occultist circles that all the terrible events since 1914 should not be ascribed to human agency but to the influence of certain demonic beings that were invisible to the eye of the average person . . . A scholar would

make himself ridiculous if he admitted he believed in the existence of demons. I myself am not a scholar and therefore can allow myself to believe in the existence of such beings.

(*Latern*, 366–7)

The Bolshevik revolution that Dr Steen claims is caused by 'ghosts' is foreseen in *Walpurgisnacht*. One of the threads of the novel is a group of workers and servants who meet under the tutelage of a Russian to imbibe the teachings of Kropotkin, Bakunin and Tolstoy. The stupendous climax (Meyrink was good at portraying cataclysmic events, see also the storm that destroys Amsterdam at the end of *The Green Face* for example) comes when these combine with the Czech nationalist forces and, driven on by 'Lucifer's Drum', rise up against the Austro-Hungarian monarchy. Meyrink had a strong antipathy towards socialism. In the few places where its supporters appear in his novels, they are negatively portrayed, for example a servant in *Walpurgisnacht* is 'a young man with a vacant expression on his face, clearly a Prague Czech, who was showing off his reading and scattering socialist slogans around such as "property is theft." ' (*Walpurgisnacht*, 100) In *The Green Face* most of the refugees after the war are not the poor, but the rich escaping higher taxes, and the intelligentsia 'whose professions no longer brought in enough to keep body and soul together'. (*Green Face*, 15) Another writer might have made a positive message out of this, a return to nature and the nobility of manual labour. In Meyrink's portrayal the language and imagery are entirely negative:

Even in the far-off days of the horrors of peace, the income of a master chimney-sweep or a pork butcher had far outstripped that of a university professor, Now, however, European society had reached that glorious stage where the old curse, "In the sweat of thy face shalt

thou eat bread" was to be understood literally ...
Muscle-power reached for the crown, whilst the products of the human brain were trodden underfoot.

(Green Face, 15)

In his notes for another, unwritten novel, he wrote, 'The
theme of the novel must be a cry of fury against the socialist
(democratic) anthill state.'

In *Walpurgisnacht* the zealots of the revolution are opposed
to the ossified remnants of the old aristocratic order, ensconced
in the Hradschin high above the left bank of the Moldau.
Meyrink's attitude was, it seems, 'a curse on both your
houses'. A few hints suggest he was equally averse to capitalism. The passage quoted above from *The Green Face* continues:

Mammon still sat on his throne, but with a look of
uncertainty on his ugly face ... And the earth was
without form and void; and darkness was upon the face
of the deep, only the spirit of the travelling salesman
could no longer move on the face of the waters as it had
done before.

(Green Face, 15)

A summary of the development of mankind in 'The Four
Moon Brethren' sees three stages, the final and most superficial being that of capitalism (with very prophetic overtones
seen from today's perspective):

In the Golden Age, when mankind was less developed,
they only believed what they could 'think', but then the
age gradually came when they only believed what they
could eat; but now they have ascended the summit of
perfection, that is, they only consider as real what they
can sell.

(Fledermäuse, 125)

Another strand in the apocalyptic thread running through this story is a pessimistic view of the mechanisation of the world, which, it suggests, has reached the point where humans themselves are becoming machines. The four moon brethren in the story of that name are four demonic beings, in human form, who hope to inherit the earth once mankind has destroyed itself. In September 1914 these four meet in the expectation that they will soon come into their kingdom and celebrate the coming annihilation of mankind in an 'apocalyptic speech', a vision of the destruction mankind is wreaking on itself through its increasing dependence on machines:

I beheld him with my own eyes, the one on the pale horse, and behind him the myriad forms of the army of machines – our friends and allies. They have long since assumed power over themselves, but mankind remains blind, still thinking themselves their masters.

Driverless locomotives, laden with boulders, come tearing along with mindless ferocity, fall on them and bury hundreds upon hundreds beneath the weight of their iron bodies.

The nitrogen in the air condenses to produce new, terrible explosives: Nature herself pushes forward, breathless in her haste to give up her best resources willingly in order to wipe out the white monster who, for millions of years, has dug scars in her face.

Metal tendrils with terrible, sharp thorns grow out of the ground . . .

Electric vipers dart along under the ground . . .

With the glowing eyes of predatory beasts the searchlights peer through the dark . . .

Sharks of steel creep round the coasts, suffocating in their bellies those who once gave life to them . . .

More and more gigantic eagles are waiting to leave the nest to circle over the last hiding places of mankind;

already thousands of iron spiders are rushing tirelessly to
and fro to weave shining silvery wings for them.

(Fledermäuse, 134–5)

It is an apocalyptic vision of the destruction of man, the
technological sorcerer, by the mechanical apprentices he has
created. It is in tune with similar attacks on the mechanisation of life by some of the Expressionist writers, for example Georg Kaiser in his plays *Gas I* and *Gas II* of 1918 and
1920. It also, like his story 'Petroleum, Petroleum' of 1902
(*Opal*, 45–51), in some ways anticipates current environmental
concerns:

And is that not a ghostly resurrection? The blood and fat
of antediluvian dragons that had long since decayed to
mineral oil resting in caverns under the earth is stirring,
wants to come back to life. Simmered and distilled in
fat-bellied cauldrons it is now petrol flowing into the
veins of new, fantastic air monsters . . . Petrol and
dragon's blood! Who can tell the difference? It is like
the demonic prelude to the Day of Judgment.

(Fledermäuse, 136)

And this from the man who claimed to have owned the
first motor car in Prague and was one of the first to dictate his
novels into a Parlograph! Even later on Meyrink showed that
he was not entirely averse to recent developments in technology as his film outlines from the 1920s (see Lube, 98) show.
Financial considerations may have been behind his proposals
for films, but his plans reveal an understanding of what was
required for effective cinema. He even seems to have antici-
pated product placement: 'Note: If necessary, instead of the
Fortuna shoe shop, the *Salamander* brand could be used, or any
other large shoe company that could be brought in for the
purposes of advertising!' (quoted by Lube, 99) In his late,

unfinished novel *The Alchemist's House*, however, film appears as one of the dubious products of Western civilisation. The sinister Dr Theen plans to use the cinema as an instrument for his 'psychopernicious arts' (*Latern*, 140). The use of modern developments to gain psychological control of society is a theme that was in the air at the time, for example in Otto Soyka's novel *Die Traumpeitsche* (The Dream Whip) of 1921.

Here, as in other places, Meyrink appears to be contradictory, on the one hand condemning technology as an example of, indeed an instrument in, Western civilisation's decline, its loss of soul, while on the other being happy to use it to the full. However, the contradiction is, at worst, venial. We have to live in the age we are born into, to reject it entirely leaves a person with serious psychological and, probably, material problems. Meyrink may have envisaged a better world, but he still had to provide for himself and his family in this one. Also, as his enquiries into spiritualism demonstrated, he had a sharp and enquiring mind, which meant that he properly understood the developments which he ultimately opposed.

In his thesis Buskirk claims that Meyrink showed little interest in the war:

> He was more and more interested in his religious search into the supernatural world and less in the society around him. While the patriotism of the First World War was inspiring easily swayed literary minds to write propaganda essays finding reasons for support of a senselessly brutal social order, Gustav Meyrink was removed emotionally from the conflict much as a Buddha.[17]

As we have seen, this is not true. Even in 1918 he was willing to use his writing in the service of his country, perhaps

[17] Buskirk, p. 28.

even to undertake some more 'confidential' assignment, and the war formed an important, though usually secondary, theme in his novels and stories. However, there is a truth in Buskirk's statement in that Meyrink *also* viewed the war from the perspective of a more profound, more 'real' spiritual reality.

At this level he was even able to take a positive message from the mass slaughter of the war. In his notes for a novel, written during the war, he wrote:

Anyone who is sensitive and still open to spiritual development could, during the time of the great war, distinctly feel powerful new forces flowing into them. They came from the many dying soldiers. Just as the buds on a tree start to sprout vigorously when the gardener prunes the branches. – The world of living beings is a large tree; most are only conscious of themselves as a single leaf, but a few make the leap into the wider consciousness of the tree and it is those who do not die, the others fall, sooner or later, like withered leaves. Thus we, who drew in new forces during the time of the great war are heir to the life of those dead warriors.

9

Meyrink in Starnberg

In 1911 Meyrink moved with his family to Starnberg, a small town at the northern end of Lake Starnberg some fifteen miles south of Munich, and stayed there for the rest of his life. He rented several houses or apartments there until he bought a house of his own in 1918. He called it the *Haus zur letzten Latern* (House by the Last Lamp). The name came from a place called the 'Wall by the Last Lamp' on the Malá Strana in Prague, on the left bank of the Moldau. It was there that he had situated the mystical house in *The Golem* where the narrator sees Pernath and Miriam after their deaths and spiritual union.

It was a large and delightful house, surrounded by trees and directly on the lake, with a glassed-in conservatory and a boathouse created by a platform over the water. Originally built in 1865, Richard Wagner had lodged there for some weeks in 1867. It became identified with Meyrink, but unfortunately he and Mena were forced to sell it in 1928 and moved out in 1929 – it is no longer standing –, but he remained in Starnberg in rented accommodation. In the contract of sale it is Meyrink's wife who is named as the owner. Was the house originally bought with his wife's money? Was it a tax dodge? An attempt to keep the house out of the claws of his creditors?

The enforced sale of the house indicates that Meyrink's financial position had worsened once more. The great success of *The Golem* led people to assume he had been able to buy the house from the profits. However, as we have seen, he sold his rights for an admittedly fairly large one-off payment, and he probably used a mortgage to pay at least part of the purchase price. He and his wife were left with almost nothing from the 79,000[1] marks for which the House by the Last Lamp was sold. 55,000 marks of the price went on some of the mortgages that had not been repaid and were taken over by the buyer, the uncle of Meyrink's son-in-law, and the Meyrinks had to use 21,000 marks of the remainder to pay off another debt on the house. A letter of 1921 to the Kurt Wolff Verlag[2] says that the unprecedented rise in living costs (this was before the galloping inflation of 1922–23) compelled him either to take out more and more mortgages on his house or to sell the rights to his books in order to get a sum which would give him the opportunity to use money to make money. He clearly took the first option, though whether he managed to 'use the money to make money' remains a moot point. Given his reputation in financial matters, it sounds unlikely.

In fact, there never seems to have been a time when he was really financially secure. There are several dunning letters in the archives, including one of 26.11.19 for a debt of 14,444 crowns (plus 6%) owed to two men (brothers?) called Schwarz going back to 1901; he apparently offered 3,000 French francs which would have been acceptable except that by the time the offer reached the creditors the rate of exchange had deteriorated. A later document mentions a debt, perhaps the same one, of 40,000 crowns in 1922.[3] In a letter of October 1925 he says he had settled that debt, but there are letters of

<hr />

[1] Around £370,000 today.

[2] Yale University Library.

[3] In 1903 14,444 Austrian crowns was the equivalent of about £600 sterling; by 1922 inflation had taken such a hold that its value was less than £1, unless the debt had been converted into Czech crowns, when it would be the equivalent of between £100 and £320 at the time.

The House by the Last Lamp

March 1925 with a lawyer representing him in a claim for payment against him by a different person. His financial situation seems to have been precarious ever since the collapse of his bank in 1902 and at various times he was clearly compelled to resort to non-literary ways of making money. In 1907 he wrote to Alfred Kubin: 'By the way, you wouldn't happen to know of a collector of Japanese art? My two ivory reliefs have just been assessed as very valuable and I'd quite like to realise them.'[4] It sounds as if he and his wife were selling off their valuables, as was also suggested by a letter to an acquaintance, Fräulein Kanoldt, around 1915: 'The chain would be very cheap at 18 marks (too fine for us).' However, the next sentence sounds more as if he were setting up a small, private jewellery business: 'Thinner ones at 7, 8, 9 (red gold).' In another letter to her he appears to be dealing in precious stones: 'Unfortunately cheap brilliants are unobtainable at the moment. The cheapest are those at 10 marks (for us), which you had earlier. In a shop these would cost at least 18–20 marks.'[5] A letter to a Herr Weber of 1914 mentions an order for 500 cigars; it sounds as if Meyrink is sending a sample. These commercial activities – how many are there unrecorded? – do lend weight to the suggestion that he worked as an agent for a champagne factory in Vienna after he left Prague.

In the archives are also records of loans and grants he was made by institutions such as the Writers' Association, for example a letter of 9.6.15 to Kurt Martens[6] thanking him for 300 marks sent by some committee. One letter to Meyrink of 15.4.1925 included a cheque for 'only 500 marks'; the writer, the editor of the *Oltener Tagblatt*, said, 'I am YOU and therefore financial matters, or the Earth Spirit, are of *no account*

[4] Letter in the Kubin Archive, Lenbachhaus.
[5] Letter in Munich City Library.
[6] Letter in Munich City Library.

whatsoever between us. *Everything that belongs to me, belongs to you. Nothing* belongs to me alone. Everything to you.' It sounds as if they were fellow members of some mystical brotherhood, or perhaps the writer regarded Meyrink as his guru.

He was also forced to write pieces he knew he could sell easily. From the middle of the 1920s onwards he wrote frequent stories and articles for popular magazines, for example *Sport im Bild* (Sport in the Picture), and also many different daily papers. Some of these, about a dozen, are stories of the fantastic. They are short, between five and seven pages in book publication, which suggests Meyrink was working to a set length. Typically for Meyrink, they contain aspects of the occult, but they are clearly written for the amusement of the reader, rather than with any literary ambition. 'Die Frau ohne Mund' (The Woman without a Mouth, *Latern*, 197–202) is about a man possessed by the spirit of a woman without a mouth. He consults a cocaine-sniffing negro from Haiti who reveals it is the spirit of a mulatto woman who was the man's mistress and died in a car crash. She has now taken possession of him by voodoo magic. Others are amusing trifles on topical themes. 'Der Jazz-Vogel' (The Jazz Bird, *Latern*, 192–6) has another negro who is on the trail of the primal sound. He finds it; it is not, however, the primal sound of creation, but of destruction. The result is jazz. 'Der schwarze Habicht' (Black Hawk, *Fledermäuse*, 174–8) is a fantasy on Sir Malcolm Campbell's land speed records in which the devil shows Meyrink an image of Black Hawk, Campbell's rival's car, and Campbell himself appears. Or is it the devil? Meyrink could write to order when financial pressure – or the devil? – drove.

More numerous are his newspaper articles of the period. They are on occult themes, either compilations from his almost encyclopaedic knowledge or accounts of his own experiences. There are over a dozen with subjects ranging from the personal – 'Meine merkwürdigste Vision' (My Most Remarkable Vision, *Latern*, 282–5) or 'How I Tried to Make

Gold in Prague' – or aspects of the occult, for example 'Hashish and Clairvoyance', 'Magic and Chance' and others on topics such as immortality, alchemy, tantric yoga, which are interesting for his biography as an adept of the occult.

With all these various sources of income the Meyrinks clearly kept body and soul together, but never managed to extricate themselves entirely from the financial mire. (Unfortunately, there is no evidence as to how they managed during the raging inflation of 1922–23.) The stress of constantly having to count his pfennigs probably explains Meyrink's suspicious attitude towards his publishers. He sometimes talked of the one-off fee for *The Golem* as if the publisher had forced him into it, when everything suggests he was the one who insisted on it. Kurt Wolff seems to have treated him very well, bringing out a six-volume 'Collected Works' in 1917, to celebrate his 50th birthday. It was during his disagreement with Kurt Wolff that he wrote 'Publishers and art dealers are always the same kind of scoundrels' and published his next novel, *The White Dominican*, with a different publisher, Rikola. The occult was not really their field, however, and for his final novel, *The Angel of the West Window*, Meyrink moved to another, Grethlein, who even bought up old stock in an attempt to revive interest in Meyrink. He received an advance of 15,000 marks; the book sold 3,500 copies. When Grethlein set the money from the sale of translation rights against the advance, even though according to the contract it should have been passed on to Meyrink, he was not pleased; he was even less pleased when Grethlein sold on his works to Schünemann Verlag, who also took over Meyrink's debts to them, a deal from which he gained nothing. As Qasim says (71), 'it was not long before Meyrink and Schünemann were arguing about the concept of "royalties";' as part of the deal, Schünemann had bought the rights to Meyrink's next – unwritten – book. Not surprisingly, it was never delivered.

After the great success of *The Golem*, Meyrink's next novel,

The Green Face sold well initially, 90,000 in the first year. Sales probably dipped because of the anti-Meyrink campaign of 1917, but perhaps not as much as Meyrink suggested; sales figures for 1925 are *The Golem* 222,000 copies, *The Green Face* 150,000, *Walpurgisncht* 120,000 and *The White Dominican* 60,000. His last novel, however, *The Angel of the West Window*, published in 1927, had only sold 2,860 copies by 1931. In the later 1920s Meyrink's main source of income – assuming he was not still dabbling in precious stones or currency speculation – apart from the articles for the popular press already mentioned, was a certain amount of translation work from English: *Japanische Geistergeschichten* (presumably *Japanese Fairy Tales*) by Lafcadio Hearn; *My First 2000 Years: The Autobiography of the Wandering Jew* by George Sylvester Viereck and P. Eldridge; two volumes of stories by Kipling and Ludwig Lewisohn's *Das Erbe im Blut* (*The Island Within*).

He also made make efforts to promote his writings and look for work. G. R. S. Mead wrote suggesting 'some [English] novels of the kind you require to translate' and a German publisher wrote to tell him where the English translation of Lion Feuchtwanger's *Jew Süss* had been published. Presumably Meyrink was looking for an English-language publisher for his own novels. In another letter he offered his services as a literary translator and as an agent at what seems the somewhat exorbitant rate of 25%.

It was as a resident of Starnberg that Meyrink decided to change his name officially from Meyer to Meyrink. What prompted the decision? Did he want to bask in the glory of being, at that time, one of the most widely publicised writers in Germany? Was he simply tired of locals asking him, 'And what is it you do for a living, Herr Meyer?'[7] Krell also reports that he kept a silver cup he had won at rowing on his desk

[7] Krell, p. 44.

with, in it, a cutting from the local newspaper: 'Few of our readers will know that our club captain is a talented writer.' Though Meyrink had no false modesty about his achievements as a writer and, as we have seen in other contexts, could be touchy if he felt his honour had been impugned, he does not seem to be the kind of person who would deliberately court the admiration of his neighbours. Perhaps his mischievous side enjoyed the idea of letting the good citizens of Starnberg know that living amongst them was the man who had mercilessly satirised them in 'The German Bourgeois' Magic Horn'? Whatever the reason, he was proud of what was associated with the name of Meyrink. When, two years later, in 1919, the aristocratic family of his father offered to have him officially adopted into the Varnbüler family, Meyrink refused. His name as a writer was nobility enough. (Frank, 10)

If a desire to make it clear that the celebrated writer, Gustav Meyrink, and the keen rower, Herr Meyer, were one and the same person, was behind the change, he might have taken a different decision one year later. His application had presumably been made early in 1917 or, more probably given the speed at which the mills of state administration grind, in 1916; the royal assent was dated 8 July 1917. The first volley in the attack which was to lead to the nationalist campaign against Meyrink came in the June 1917 issue of the magazine *Bühne und Welt*. Once the waves had reached local tradesmen and labourers, Meyrink may well have preferred the anonymity of simple Herr Meyer.

Meyrink's early incarnation as a dandy in Prague was, at least in part, a pose he adopted *pour épater le bourgeois*. The rather superior, aristocratic-looking gentleman certainly has the look of a protective shell. Later, when as an established writer he moved in the literary/artistic café society of Prague, Vienna and Munich, he no longer needed a mask to hide behind. He did not, however adopt the Bohemian style of his fellow coffee house frequenters. Despite his sociable nature, he still stood somewhat apart from those around him; Qasim (63) calls him at this time an 'outsider within a group of outsiders.' But what set him apart from the others was not a pose but his real self, the man who, as his friend Roda Roda put it, 'through the wisdom of the Orient and the Occident had thought his way up into a higher sphere of understanding, far from reality'.

As he grew older, he evidently became more comfortable with himself, so much so, that when he was settled in Starnberg he felt no need to distinguish himself outwardly from the bourgeois he had deliberately tried to shock. Part of this was doubtless due to his marriage to Mena Meyrink and his 'very happy family life'[8] contributed to the image of bourgeois normality. (Oddly enough, the few recorded comments by Meyrink on marriage are negative. There are notes for a 'Book of Poisons' in the archive. Although hashish is included, the other 'poisons' are social and psychological: alongside 'money' and 'kitsch writers' is 'marriage, love etc.'.)

Visitors and friends frequently commented on the contrast between the fantastic nature of what he wrote and talked about and the ordinariness of his appearance. Max Brod remarked that his 'clear business hand' and his 'banal purple ink' were completely at odds with the things going on around him. Ripellino misused Brod's words, suggesting the 'banal' applied to Meyrink's writings as well as to the ink in which they were written.[9] Gershom Scholem, who visited Meyrink in Starnberg in 1921, commented that his 'ordinary appearance (he looked like the lowliest petit bourgeois) contrasted with the fantastic stories he wrote.'[10] The Viennese journalist Francis, who visited him in the year before he died, said:

[8] Mangoldt, p. 99.

[9] Ripellino, p. 31

[10] Scholem, p. 134.

Meyrink in his car with his son and daughter, early 1920s

the author of *The Golem, The Green Face* and *The White Dominican* did not in the least resemble the descriptions that have been given of him . . . This German Edgar Allan Poe had the noble appearance of a country gentleman.[11]

The contradiction between his outer appearance and his inner life had always been something that struck those who knew him. He did not feel the need to make a show of the spiritual concerns with which he was occupied. In Starnberg it was the very ordinariness of his outward appearance which contrasted with the extraordinary inner life he led.

His novels after the War: The White Dominican

In 1917 Julius Bab prophesied:

Even if *The Golem* and *The Green Face* should turn out to be relatively short-lived, the author of 'The German Bourgeois' Magic Horn' is sure to live on as a considerable and highly original writer of prose.[12]

To a certain extent, Bab's prophecy has proved well-founded. Despite the continuing popularity of *The Golem*, it is on his satirical short stories that his reputation still largely rests in Germany. Opinions on his novels, on the other hand, vary widely. There are those who see them as an important part in German literature of the first quarter of the twentieth century. For others their importance lies in the spiritual message they convey. Then there are those who dismiss them as

---

[11] Francis, 6.12.1932.
[12] Quoted in: Böttcher, afterword to *Des Deutschen Spießers Wunderhorn*, pp. 272–3.

popular fiction with a sensationalist streak. The attitude of the majority is probably a combination of all three. Nowhere, however, do opinions differ more widely than on the first novel he published after the war, *The White Dominican* (1921). For Gérard Heym it is not just 'a good story', it is 'the most profound of Meyrink's novels and also the most "authentic";'[13] and for Raymond Abellio it is simply Meyrink's 'chef d'oeuvre'.[14] For Jan Christof Meister, on the other hand, it is a 'tract with minimal literary packaging'[15] and Lube calls it a mixture of 'trashy plot and theoretical tract.'[16]

The process of initiation which the hero, Christopher Dovecote, undergoes, culminating in the immortality of a purified body and union with the feminine principle, is based on Taoism, which was relatively unknown in the West at the time. According to Gérard Heym, himself an adept and extremely well versed in occult traditions, Meyrink came across the Tao in books written in the later 19th century by an Austrian Sinologist, August Pfitzmaier (who, according to Heym, was quietly encouraged by his academic masters to choose other, less fantastic subjects in future). Heym says that he was told by friends of Meyrink that Pfitzmaier's articles filled him with such enthusiasm that 'he immediately tried to get into contact with the ancient tradition by clairvoyance. More than that, he managed to identify with it to the point where he was able to penetrate the secrets of the tradition.'[17]

---

[13] Gérard Heym in his introduction to the French translation of *The White Dominican*, reprinted in Caroutch, p. 162.

[14] Raymond Abellio: 'La Nuit de Walpurgis', in Caroutch, p.155.

[15] Jan Christof Meister: *Hypostasierung. Die Logik mythischen Denkens im Werk Gustav Meyrinks nach 1907*, Frankfurt/M., Bern, 1987, p. 253.

[16] Manfred Lube: 'Gustav Meyrink als Literat in Prag, Wien und München', *Phaicon* no. 3, p. 87.

[17] Heym, p. 162.

Christopher Dovecote follows a path of the Tao called *Shi Kiai* and *Kieu Kiai* (the dissolution with – sometimes 'of' – the sword). This is a path of transformation, not unlike a mystical interpretation of European alchemy, by which the physical body is transmuted into an immortal spiritual body. This is one of the causes of lack of action in the novel, since part of this 'way' is for the initiate to remain inactive and 'turn cold' in order to 'spiritualise' every last cell of his physical form. (*White Dominican*, 132–5)

Despite the criticism of official Christianity in the novel, including the exposure of the false spirituality of a Christian miracle worker, it does contain an attempt to merge the Chinese and Christian esoteric traditions. The name of the hero and his age at death/transfiguration associate him with Christ, and the White Dominican of the title is both a legendary figure associated with the local church and a Master of the mystical order Christopher Dovecote joins after his metamorphosis; Heym also suggests the name reflects an exclusive Buddhist order of White Monks.[18] The hero's father and the local chaplain are represented as following two parallel, rather than opposing, spiritual paths. A further tradition evoked is that of Freemasonry, which is said to have preserved certain mysteries, though without understanding their inner significance (perhaps a leftover from the freemasonry novel he was commissioned to write during the war). Both in its imagery and message, *The White Dominican* avoids the sectarian approach of suggesting one spiritual tradition possesses the key to immortal life, but it presents the path of the Tao as the one that has succumbed least to the externalisation of its symbols and rituals.

[18] Heym, p. 165.

The Angel of the West Window

The first question that presents itself when considering Meyrink's final novel, *The Angel of the West Window* (1927), is whether it is by Meyrink at all. When J. P. Strelka published a Meyrink anthology under the title of *Der Engel vom westlichen Fenster*, he received a letter from F. A. Schmid Noerr:

> Allow me to describe briefly how 'Baphomet', the original title, came to be written. In an antiquarian bookshop in Munich I had found a little brochure about the life of John Dee. I took it to my friend Meyrink, who was very ill at the time, and offered it him as material for a novel. Meyrink read it, thought it was marvellous, but admitted, 'I don't think I can manage that now; would you like to do it? Herr von Günther, the editor at Grethlein-Verlag, has asked me to let him have a novel, 15,000 marks advance, unseen. We could earn a tidy sum.' You will already have guessed what happened: Meyrink, the more successful writer, gave his name, I wrote the novel from A to Z and we each got 7,500 marks . . . But one day, when I read some of my manuscript to him, he said, almost horrified, 'That's impossible, that's your own personal style, no one will believe I've written that.' In particular he objected to the poems I'd inserted, saying he'd never even been able to rhyme *Herz* with *Schmerz* . . . Finally we drew up a contract in which Meyrink and his wife agreed to pass on to me half of all the income from the novel . . . I would also like to point out that I wrote the *Goldmachergeschichten* (Stories of the Makers of Gold) . . . that brought each of us 2,500 marks.[19]

---

[19] Letter of 20.11.1966, quoted in Smit, pp. 243–5.

It is generally accepted that Schmid Noerr was involved in the writing of *The Angel of the West Window*, but did he write 'the whole novel from A to Z'? According to Meister,[20] Schmid Noerr's various statements about his authorship were contradictory. He is said to have told one acquaintance that the parts involving Emperor Rudolf in Prague were by him, while claiming to Eduard Frank to have contributed ninety per cent of the book. Meyrink's long-standing ill-health did cause him greater problems towards the end of his life; on the other hand he was working on another novel, 'The Alchemist's House', so there is no reason to believe he would feel absolutely incapable of writing a novel on John Dee, or at least collaborating on one. Max Brod mentions that Meyrink's extensive library in Prague, from which he was allowed to borrow books, contained works by Carl Kiesewetter, the author of the 'brochure' on John Dee, though he does not say whether that specific work was there.

Meyrink's continuing financial problems make Schmid Noerr's claim seem a possibility. It is generally accepted that he wrote the 'Stories of the Makers of Gold' (recently republished in paperback under Meyrink's name in a collection together with genuine Meyrink stories[21]) and some of the poems in *The Angel of the West Window* were published in a collection of his poetry. On the other hand, Schmid Noerr published a 442-page historical novel of his own, *Frau Perchtas Auszug. Ein mythischer Roman* (Frau Perchta's Departure. A Mythical Novel) only one year after *The Angel of the West Window*, which makes his claim to sole authorship of the latter dubious. Pritzky, in *Die Literatur* of 1925 presented a collection of purple passages from 'Stories of the Makers of Gold' which are so awful – he described them as well below the standard of the contemporary equivalent of Mills and

[20] Meister, p. 226
[21] *Der Mönch Laskaris*, 2004.

Boon — that it seems impossible Schmid Noerr could have written the whole of *The Angel*.[22]

Since Schmid Noerr's revelation, scholars have generally assumed Meyrink's 'last novel' is the result of a collaboration and stylistic analyses have been done to suggest which parts might be by each author.[23] While the precise percentage of Meyrink's own contribution remains undecided, *The Angel of the West Window* is a richly textured novel which is worthy to stand as a fictional summation of his preoccupation with the occult. Gershom Scholem for example, who considered his usage of the Cabbala in *The Golem* dubious, called it a 'profoundly mystical novel'.[24]

The Alchemist's House

What has survived of 'The Alchemist's House', the novel that was left unfinished at Meyrink's death, is three chapters, taking eighty pages in the published version, and a twenty-page outline of the whole novel containing remarks on style and language, the time and place of the setting, the characters and the plot (*Latern*, pp. 41–143).

The house of the title is an ancient building in which, according to legend, an alchemist called Gustenhöver (also spelt 'Gustenhöwer') once lived. Not unlike many of the buildings in the Prague ghetto, 'in the course of the centuries it had frequently been altered, partly pulled down and rebuilt'. It belongs to Hieronymus Gustenhöver, a clockmaker and

---

[22] Meister quotes some, pp. 356–7.

[23] See for example Michael Mitchell: 'Gustav Meyrink' in: *Major Figures of Austrian Literature: The Interwar Years 1918–1938*, ed. Donald G. Daviau, Riverside, pp. 286–288; Meister pp. 227–35.

[24] Scholem, p. 135; for the historical John Dee see Woolley: *The Queen's Conjuror*, London 2001.

descendent of the alchemist. The central character is Dr Steen, whose main field of interest is psychoanalysis. He has an almost magical attraction for women, who 'go wild about him', and no conscience: 'he eradicated it years ago by psychoanalysis'. He does not use his psychoanalytical expertise for the good of others 'but, on the contrary, to *arouse* "complexes" − psychological confusion − in his victims'. Like a villain in a James Bond story, he has plans to rule the whole world, by making a film in which he himself will play the Yazidi demiurge, Malak Ta'us ('Peacock Angel' − one possible title of the novel is 'At the sign of the Peacock'), whom so far only Yazidi initiates have seen and whom he resembles. He hopes this image 'will impress itself on the minds of sensitive souls and make them receptive to demonic insinuation.' Steen, however, has given his watch, which stopped working while he was a child, to Gustenhöver to be repaired; when, after many fruitless attempts, it is mended, Steen's conscience suddenly returns. A late Meyrink story, 'Der Uhrmacher' (The Clockmaker), which was published in *Simplicissimus* in 1926, is based on a similar parallel between a person's clock and their mind. Arnold Keyserling saw this little story (twelve pages in length) as a portrayal of 'the personal way, the initiation of Gustav Meyrink', calling it, in the title of his short book, 'the metaphysics of the clockmaker'.[25]

His Attitude to Literature

After 1916 and the publication of the anthology *Bats*, Meyrink had abandoned the short story in favour of the novel. In the first years after the war the flow of novels dried up, apart from *The White Dominican*, and he concentrated on editing books

[25] Arnold Keyserling: *Die Metaphysik des Uhrmachers von Gustav Meyrink*, Vienna, 1966.

with spiritual and occult themes. He managed to persuade
Rikola, who published *The White Dominican*, to embark on a
series of 'Novels and Books of Magic', which he edited and
for which he wrote introductions. Five appeared between
1921 and 1924 before Rikola decided to pull out. Three are
novels, two by Franz Spunda, a German practitioner of the
'magic novel' and one, *Dhoula Bel* translated by Meyrink, by
the mulatto American Rosicrucian and practitioner of sexual
magic, P. B. Randolph. Meyrink's introduction to this novel is,
apparently, the source of the presumably apocryphal story that
Randolph tried to kill Madame Blavatsky, who was in India,
by teleportation of a pistol. He says a friend told him:

> It was in Adyar (India). Madame Blavatsky and I were
> sitting, motionless and silent, on our chairs under large
> parasols, for it was swelteringly hot. Suddenly Madame
> Blavatsky cried out, 'Now he's shooting at me, the nigger.
> Ah, now the devil's come for him.'
>
> At my astonished question as to what was the matter,
> she said that Randolph had just tried to kill her by
> magic. He had loaded a pistol (in America! Thousands
> of miles away!) commanding that the bullet he would
> fire should dematerialise and rematerialise as lead in her
> heart. At the last moment, however, Randolph had gone
> mad and shot himself in the forehead.
>
> (*Fledermäuse*, 359–60)

The other two books in the series are more serious works
on spiritual and occult matters. One is on the Hindu saint
Ramakrishna, who tried to demonstrate the essential unity of
all religions. This presumably appealed to Meyrink who himself found similar patterns in different religious traditions. The
other was a biography of the 19th-century French occultist,
Eliphas Levi.

In this period Meyrink edited two other books which

reflected his personal interests, but for different publishers. One was his translation of Thomas Aquinas's treatise on the philosopher's stone; the other, *Das Buch vom lebendigen Gott* (The Book of the Living God, 1919), was by a German mystic and painter, Joseph Anton Schneiderfranken, who published his books under the name of Bô Yin Râ.

Schneiderfranken was a painter whose many mystical writings were – and still are – popular. He and Meyrink first met in 1917 and the attraction seems to have been immediate for two men with a very similar outlook on life. 'I would not have written this preface,' Meyrink wrote, 'if, before I met the author, I had not, myself and alone, found confirmed everything that is in his book.' (*Fledermäuse*, 380) The admiration was mutual. Schneiderfranken wrote a glowing celebration of the author of *The Golem*:

> *Gustav Meyrink's* life is the life of a *true* mystic of our days, an *occultist* who is *truly* at home in the occult, an *initiate* who can genuinely say of himself that the oldest mysteries of the world hold no secret for him. Only *such* a man could write the *mystical novels* that *Gustav Meyrink* has given us.
>
> (*Fledermäuse*, 391)

The friendship cooled and a year after Meyrink's death Schneiderfranken published an article distancing himself from him. He pointed out that passages from the chapter 'In the Mirror' in *Walpurgisnacht* were clearly based on his own writings. His objection was not to Meyrink's use of his work, but to the manner in which it was done, namely that his ideas had been used simply as *literary material*, rather than for their value as occult teachings. Schneiderfranken claimed that Meyrink had:

> several times told him that he did not dream of regarding

the teachings and experiences dealt with in his occult novels as true . . . as a novelist he reserved the right to use material that particularly appealed to him . . . He wanted to be judged not as a teacher of occult or mystical ideas, but as an artist.

(Fledermäuse, 394–5)

Schneiderfranken's description partly echoes the assessment of Gershom Scholem, who said:

Thus I went out to Starnberg in 1921 with a certain amount of curiosity and made the acquaintance of a man in whom deep-rooted mystical convictions and literarily exploited charlatanry were almost inextricably amalgamated.[26]

Scholem called the Jewish mysticism in *The Golem* and *The Green Face* 'pseudo-Kabbala' and described how Meyrink read out passages from his novels saying, 'I did write this, but I don't know what it means.'

Whether Meyrink commented on his use of occult material as cynically as Schneiderfranken suggested or whether the latter misunderstood the precise meaning of what his friend was saying is, of course, uncertain, but both are possible because Meyrink's comments on his work as a writer are contradictory. On the one hand he could insist that he was a literary artist. The outline for *The Alchemist's House* includes descriptions of technical details needed to create a 'complete work of art'. (*Latern*, 125) More realistically, he could insist that, 'A work of art needs to be sold if it is not to sit resplendent, alone on an icy peak.'[27]

On the other hand, in a 'self-description' written in the

---

[26] Scholem, p. 133.
[27] 'München als Kunststadt' in: *Der Zwiebelfisch*, 1926/28., p. 25.

mid-1920s he insists that his novels and stories have nothing to do with literature and everything to do with occult teachings. Speaking of himself in the third person, he says:

> Attitude to literature as art: none. He maintains that his own works have hardly anything to do with it. He says that what he writes is 'magic' – suggestion – and not bound to the recipes and rules of artistic structure, that it has very little in common with what the professors of all categories understand by 'art' and literature.[28]

And yet the outline of *The Alchemist's House* contains a number of precisely such 'recipes and rules':

> A varied and developing *plot alone* cannot in my opinion give a novel the tension it must have if it wants to be seen as a complete work of art; also required is description that is original, full of atmosphere, lively, optically effective and so gripping that it holds the reader in its spell from the first to the last sentence.
>
> (*Latern*, 125)

But this concentration on the technical aspects of composition does not preclude the novel from containing a message, though the message must not come across as such, but as a legitimate part of the novel:

> A further ingredient of a work of art is – at least this is my opinion – that a hidden, cosmic deeper meaning should underlie the plot and the characters involved in it. Naturally this meaning should only become evident

---

[28] 'Selbstbeschreibung des Autors Gustav Meyrink' in: *Der Zwiebelfisch*, 1926, p. 25; quoted from manuscript in *Meyrinkiana*.

to the sensitive reader; *the deeper meaning should never be obtrusive.*

(*Latern*, 125)

A more open version of this is Meyrink's response to the accusation that his *Simplicissimus* stories did not take the occult seriously:

I readily admit that my stories in the 'Magic Horn' could lead people to assume I was just playing with metaphysical problems, for who could know the reasons why I wrote for *Simplicissimus* all those years ago. From childhood I was deeply convinced of the existence of a 'world beyond' and the last thing I would do would be to make fun of that kind of thing. Putting on a mask was a ruse; I wanted to infiltrate *Simplicissimus* in order to have a platform from which I could get my sacred cause across to the public, from behind, so to speak.[29]

As far as his early stories are concerned, this sounds very much like wisdom after the event. He did include things that interested him and were important to him in his stories but not, I think, acting as a kind of secret agent for the occult at that stage. Later on, however, he even, on a couple of occasions, claimed he was acting as a kind of amanuensis for some outside force. One example is the opening of *The White Dominican*, where his claim to be 'merely some kind of receiver for supernatural communications' (*Dominican*, 15) can be regarded as a literary device. Different is the bizarre story he told Ursula von Mangoldt:

He was working on *The Green Face* when, suddenly, he

---

[29] From an unpublished article 'Dem Andenken Gustav Meyrinks' by K. G. Bittner quoted in Frank, 14.

saw a large boot underneath his bed. When, in his wak-
ing dream, he bent down to pull it out, he saw a horrify-
ingly ugly little Jew with red hair, runny eyes and curled
sidelocks. Then a second, a third, a fourth. 'You must
give me something,' the red-haired Jew said. Meyrink
took out his wallet and gave it to him. 'You must give
me something more,' the little Jew said. – And now
Meyrink's eyes started to shine as he went on with his
story: 'I was overcome with such boundless pity and such
genuine love for this little chap that I grasped my heart
to give it to him. At that I heard a voice saying, "His
name will be written in the Book of Life." ' And he saw
a book written from right to left in the Jewish manner
and his name shone out from it. 'Now you must do
something else,' the little Jew went on. 'You must write
something about the Jews in your novel.' And Meyrink
wrote the chapter about Egyolk, that was dictated to
him word for word by the little chap, and then arranged
the other chapters of *The Green Face* round it.[30]

Perhaps Meyrink did sometimes write in a kind of trance,
but there is no doubt that the message behind his novels and
the stories in *Bats* was one that concerned him deeply. But
there is still some truth in the comments by Schneiderfranken
and Scholem. He chose material for his stories and novels
which appealed to him and seemed effective, both in the literary sense and as a vehicle for his own ideas. How far he
believed in the *specific* details of alchemy or the *Shi Kiai* and
Kieu Kiai of the Tao is irrelevant. It is the 'deeper meaning'
underlying them that was important to him.

[30] Mangoldt, pp. 96–7.

10

Meyrink's Beliefs

Meyrink was christened in the Protestant church in Maria-hilferstrasse in Vienna. What part religion – the Christian religion – played in his upbringing, apart from obligatory lessons at school, is unknown. It certainly plays relatively little part in his writings. The concept of sin and the need for redemption is completely absent and the idea of a God somewhere above the world is rare and does not really seem to impinge on his personal beliefs. Christianity is virtually absent from his articles, and when it appears in his stories and novels, it is often shown in a negative light, for example in the conventicle in *The Green Face* and the fraudulent miracle-worker in *The White Dominican*, or, from his early pieces, the figure of the pastor, significantly called 'Dr Simulans', in 'Die Geschichte vom Löwen Alois' (The Story of Alois the Lion) and the infamous 'clergywives' in 'The Ring of Saturn', not to mention the Englishwomen in *The Alchemist's House* 'with their Liberty-silk views of the dear Lord' who are outraged at the idea of people being allowed to play cards on Sundays, 'the mornings of which should be reserved for prayer, the afternoons for procreation'.

In 1927 he officially left the Church and declared himself a 'Buddhist of the Northern School' as he says in his 'Self-description'. What exactly he meant by 'Buddhist *of the North-ern School*' is unclear. This was a branch of Zen Buddhism that was important in the 7th century, but declined soon after and by the modern age was certainly no longer a living tradition. Perhaps it was another of Meyrink's mystifications. However, its decline was due to political rather than philosophical issues, in particular it was attacked by its enemies for promoting '*gradual* enlightenment'; it may be this feature that Meyrink had in mind when he declared himself a follower of the School.

The key is his devotion to yoga, which he practised from the mid-1890s until the end of his life. His beliefs regarding the nature of humanity correspond fairly closely to those informing the teachings of yoga, although the specific details vary from time to time, as he made what he saw as new discoveries. Basically for Meyrink there is the physical body and a spiritual essence; they are both part of the person. He insists that the spiritual does not come from some other realm, from a 'world beyond', but is part of the same material world as the physical body, only not perceptible to our normal senses. Occultism, he says is 'meta-physics' (ie what another writer calls 'transcendental physics'), that is beyond normal physics, but only:

insofar as its phenomena transcend the limits of current knowledge about the way the laws of nature work. Its 'spirits' and 'ghosts' are just as material as human bodies, they belong to the realm of the material just as much as X-rays[1]

The occult world is not so much 'beyond' as 'beyond our physical senses'. Later in the same essay he uses Johann Zöllner's theory of a fourth dimension to explain why there are phenomena our senses cannot detect.[2]

This conviction that there is a spiritual dimension to reality

---

[1] 'An der Grenze des Jenseits' (On the Threshold of the World Beyond'), *Latern*, p. 373.

[2] Johann Zöllner, tr. Massey: *Transcendental Physics*, London, 1882.

was the basis of Meyrink's beliefs. In both 'On the Threshold of the World Beyond' of 1923, and 'The Transformation of the Blood', written in 1927–28, he takes this idea one step further, in a way that has parallels in Buddhist traditions: 'Objective reality does not exist, only subjective,' (*Latern*, 392) and 'everything we think we perceive here on earth and in the material cosmos as existing objectively outside us is not material, but a state of our own self.' (*Fledermäuse*, 215)

The importance of this is not so much in the precise nature of reality but in his view of the self. We should look inside, not outside; the forces we need to activate are within us, not outside. The curse of modern man for Meyrink is his split consciousness. The purpose of spiritual exercises such as meditation and yoga is to open ourselves up to what is *inside* us and the ultimate goal is union – union with ourselves. There is an everyday self and a spiritual self, though most people go through their lives unaware of the latter. Meyrink came to realise that what he called the 'Masked Figure' or the 'Pilot' was not some external, spiritual being, but his other self:

> the outer person is separated from the inner, hidden person, the Masked Figure, who is alien, totally alien to us in our everyday consciousness . . . I realised that the purpose of *my* life was to achieve union with the 'Masked Figure' . . . consciously and instinctively.
>
> (*Fledermäuse*, 271)

The idea of union, though not in precisely the same terms, is central to yoga. Meyrink's further explanation initially sounds bizarre, but he does insist he is putting it in figurative terms:

> in a way the Masked Figure is standing upright within us, it is the spinal cord – the susumna, which is what yoga is truly about. The outer person is separated from it

211

because it is standing at an angle – in some way or other
'at an angle' to the masked Figure. That is why they do
not coincide.

(*Fledermäuse, 271*)

The passage recalls a conversation which rather baffled
Gershom Scholem:

Suddenly, without preliminaries, he asked me: 'Do you
know where God dwells?' It was hardly possible to give
a precise answer to such a question, unless one wanted to
quote the famous Rabbi Mendel of Kozk: Wherever
one lets him in. Meyrink gave me a penetrating look and
said: 'In the spinal cord'. This was new to me, and thus I
made my first acquaintance with the famous Yoga work
The Serpent Power by Sir John Woodroffe, alias Richard
[actually Arthur] Avalon. Meyrink probably owned the
only copy existent in Germany at the time.[3]

Given his spinal problems, it is perhaps not surprising that
Meyrink should be susceptible to the Hindu concept of
Kundalini, of spiritual power coiled like a snake at the base of
the spine. His identification of it with God is unusual for him,
as that is a term he generally avoids. In Hinduism, *kundalini*
is 'the divine within' and one might expect him to see that
as the spiritual self, rather than something external to the
individual; perhaps Scholem interpreted what Meyrink was
saying as referring to God. Scholem visited him in 1921. In
the later, 'figurative' use of the idea quoted above, Meyrink
incorporated the Hindu teaching of various 'subtle bodies'
into his own view of man as having an 'outer person' and an
'inner person'.

[3] Scholem, p. 134.

In this view death is not the end, but the beginning, it is not the destruction of the self, but its release. Answering the question, 'Is there such a thing as immortality?' he said, 'there is nothing else, nothing other than immortality alone. Life and immortality are the same. What the ordinary man understands by death does not exist.' (*Fledermäuse*, 291) The death of the physical body is a transition to a different, spiritual state.

Meyrink appeared to have turned his back on the Christian religion in which he had been brought up. However, a late entry in one of his notebooks – it is almost unique in being dated – describes a revelation which involves Christ:

> Today, 7 August 1930, at 10 o'clock in the morning, after a long, most harrowing night, the scales suddenly fell from my eyes and I now know what the purpose of all existence truly is.
>
> We should not change ourselves through yoga, instead we should *build* a god, so to speak or, to put it in Christian terms: 'We should not follow Christ, but take him down from the cross.'
>
> I should therefore crown the Old Man I always see in the distance, clothe him in purple and make him lord of my life. Now I do see him crowned and wearing the cloak of purple. The more perfect *he* becomes, the sooner he will help *me*. So then HE is the adept and I will only participate inasmuch as he will at some future time merge with me, for basically he is my quintessential self. 'He must increase, but I must decrease' – that is the meaning of the words of John the Baptist.
>
> (*Latern*, 346)

So did Meyrink convert back to Christianity? No. 'Christ' and the 'Old Man' have a similar function to the 'Pilot', perhaps also *kundalini*. They represent one part of him, 'his quintessential self', and the goal is still union. The insight seems to be that until then he had assumed his inner double was perfect and it was his 'everyday' self he needed to transform to achieve union, but now the transformation is focused on his spiritual self.

Ursula von Mangoldt, reporting Albert Talhoff, suggests there was a deathbed conversion. As he was dying, she says, he suddenly had a vision:

> He called his daughter and said to her, 'Dying is hard. Death is the most transitory part of life. But see, there is only one God: Christ!' Then he lay back, smiling, and died.[4]

This is not mentioned by his wife, in her description of his death. If something of the kind did in fact happen it was surely not a deathbed conversion, but a development of the insight of 1 August 1930.

The image of union with one's double as one of the final steps on the spiritual path goes back at least to *The Golem*. When Pernath sees what Hillel calls his 'true double, *Habal Garmin*, "the breath of the bones",' he will be released from the bonds of physical reality. (*Golem*, 120) The basic process of opening oneself up to one's inner world and achieving union with one's spiritual self underlies the novels, despite the different garb in which the process is clothed in each: the Cabbala, yoga, alchemy; the *Habal Garmin*, the Baphomet, the hermaphrodite. He does use these as 'literary material' to attract and amuse his readers, but they still rest on Meyrink's deeply held personal belief. Schneiderfranken's complaint is rather contradictory in that he does admit this:

[4] Mangoldt, p. 100.

His view, he said, was that it was *simply an aesthetic requirement* that the author of a novel or short story had to give the impression he himself was convinced of the things in the material he used. It was easy for him to satisfy that requirement, he said, since he was in fact convinced of the *existence* of an occult world normally inaccessible to people, and often felt its influence when writing.

(*Fledermäuse*, 394)

The real difference between the two seems to have been that Schneiderfranken, as Bô Yin Râ, took a didactic approach to his writing, while Meyrink was well aware that for the writer of fiction 'the deeper meaning must never be too obtrusive'. (*Latern*, 125). But that did not mean he was any less sincere in his belief in that 'deeper meaning'.

11

His Death

Even Meyrink's death is the subject of a characteristic anecdote. Thomas Theodor Heine, a caricaturist who had worked for *Simplicissimus* at the same time as Meyrink, described himself as a solid materialist who did not believe in the occult. On 4 December 1932 he came across a strange fox terrier acting oddly in his garden. He tried to drive it away, but the dog stood its ground and looked at him sadly before it ran off. The look immediately made Heine think of Meyrink, whom he had not seen for years. He told his wife about the odd incident. The next day, when he heard that Meyrink had just died, he recalled how Meyrink, when they had first met, had promised that one day he would give him proof of the truth of the doctrine of the transmigration of souls.[1]

Meyrink died on 4 December 1932. The manner of his death was a fitting end for a man who had spent most of his life in pursuit of spiritual truth. For some years his health had been deteriorating with a recurrence of his diabetes and spinal problems. The official cause of his death, according to Mena Meyrink, was uraemia.

Some assume his end was hastened by the suicide of his son, Harro. The previous winter Harro had seriously injured his spine in a skiing accident; after several months of treatment it became clear he would never recover completely and would

---

[1] Thomas Theodor Heine: 'Erinnerungen and Gustav Meyrink', *Das Tagebuch* 50, 10.12.1932, p. 1967; quoted in Heisserer, pp. 28–9.

never be able to walk properly again. On 12 July, after an evening spent with the family which gave no hint of his intentions, he went out on his crutches into the woods and killed himself. According to some he shot himself, in other versions he took sleeping pills and slashed his wrists. The latter would explain the suggestions that Harro's suicide replicated that of Charousek in *The Golem*.[2] Meyrink himself, however, does not make that parallel, even though he does mention *The Golem* in connection with his son's death. As the motive for Charousek letting his blood drip into the ground is revenge, whereas by all accounts one of the reasons for Harro's suicide was so as not to be a burden to his family, the parallel is at best superficial.

It is also uncertain whether the sadness at his son's death did hasten Meyrink's end. In the immediate aftermath he wrote to a friend, Bertram van Eyck, 'A terrible misfortune has struck my family and myself and I am more dead than alive.' But a little later in the same month he wrote to a close friend, Oldrich Neubert, in a very different frame of mind:

> I have found my son and am united with him. But this union is quite, quite different from the way I previously thought it might be. If I had been told that it would happen in this way, I would have been very sad in my earthly blindness, for I would have thought it was too little. In reality, however, it is such a glorious experience you think your heart is about to burst . . . First of all I woke during the night feeling I had to drink a glass of water. I wasn't thirsty and yet it was thirst I felt, but a quite different thirst from usual. I drank a glass of water, but I had to force myself, I wasn't enjoying it. Then

---

[2] For example Mangoldt, pp. 99–100.

came the sudden awareness: my son is thirsty and I am drinking for him! . . . The next morning I suddenly knew I had to put his hat on, just as Pernath puts on the other man's hat in *The Golem*. I did it thinking, now in a way I am my son and he is me . . . All at once I had an inspiration: pray with all the fervour you can to ISIS, the Egyptian mother of the gods of whom it is said she respects neither earthly nor heavenly law, she sees neither right nor wrong. With her love she breaks every rigid law, every karma and everything. And so I turned my face towards Egypt and cried out inwardly, All-Mother Isis, work a miracle, an incomprehensible miracle for my son and my wife and my daughter . . . And soon the miracle started and it has not finished yet . . . It is as if the person I was yesterday had died and a new person had arisen. The sorrow for my son has vanished without trace. If, with a wave of the hand, I could wipe out everything that has happened, his fall while skiing and everything, I would not do it, rather I would reduce my hand to ashes in the flames.

(*Latern*, 457–9)

Whether the death of his son contributed to it or not, Meyrink knew that his end was approaching. And he was determined to approach death clearly and consciously, he wanted to *experience* death, not slip away in a drug-induced sleep. In a letter to a friend just over a year after he died, his wife described his last night:

For us the death of my husband – I call this grandeur of dying resurrection – was a high mass of religion and grandeur. Since the devastating shock of the death of our beloved boy, Gustl had lost the will to live – his spirit already longed to be on the other side – his eyes grew ever more radiant, his body less and less. – All this

219

time he didn't talk much at all – he sat there, rapt, his gaze on distant shores. On 2 December at 11 o'clock at night, he said to me, these are his words, 'I'm going to die now, please don't try to persuade me not to, the release is much too great and important – and please, however much I suffer, do not give me any sedatives – I want to be upright and conscious as I cross over.' – And that was how he waited for death to come: upright, clear, without complaining, without whining. His eyes grew ever more radiant and at 7.30 on the morning of Sunday 4 December he drew his last breath. We were deeply moved by joy that his spirit freed itself so harmoniously. His body remained behind, like a chrysalis – the butter-fly has flown up to the heights – Just as he remained upright in his death – so have I remained upright. His death and also the death of my boy, he, too, went on his way with his head held high – almost with joy. – They are an example telling me that there is nothing to be frightened of about death. – Despite the harrowing blows I am so rich! – Nothing and no one can take away the inner riches Gustl gave me. I am so strangely joyfully united with them 'on the other side' and happy that every day brings me closer to them.

(*Latern*, 464)

Meyrink approached his death almost as if it was the ulti-mate in yoga exercises. He was concerned that yoga had so strengthened his body that he might be buried alive and asked that the doctor should stab him in the heart to make sure he was dead. (*Fledermäuse*, 418) His desire to experience his own death consciously was the logical conclusion of a life spent exploring the idea that death was not the end, but a transfer to another state. He went to his death in the belief that the final words on Hauberrisser in *The Green Face* would also apply to him:

He was a living man
Both here and beyond.

That is the message of the inscription on his gravestone
in Starnberg:

V I
V O

INDEX

Books by Gustav Meyrink available from Dedalus:

The five novels translated by Mike Mitchell:

The Golem
The Green Face
Walpurgisnacht
The White Dominican
The Angel of the West Window

A collection of short stories translated by Maurice Raraty:

The Opal (and other Stories)

These books can be bought from your local bookshop, online from amazon.co.uk or direct from Dedalus by post. Please write to **Cash sales, Dedalus Limited, 24–26, St Judith's Lane, Sawtry, Cambs, PE28 5XE.** For further details of the Dedalus list please go to our website http://www. dedalusbooks.com or write to us for a catalogue.